PRENTICE HALL B

# Guided Practice Activities

PEARSON

Prentice
Hall

Needham, Massachusetts
Upper Saddle River, New Jersey

4 5 6 7 8 9 10    08 07 06

ISBN 0-13-116473-2

# Table of Contents

# Dear Parents and Guardians:

¡Saludos!

Greetings and welcome to Level B of *REALIDADES*. Your child has already learned what it is like to be in a foreign language class, just as you have learned how to help your child succeed in this endeavor. Your child has already begun to understand, speak, read, and write Spanish, and explored various Spanish-speaking cultures. No doubt, you and your child have also discovered that language learning is a building process that requires considerable time and practice, but also that it is one of the most rewarding things your child can learn in school.

Language learning calls on all of the senses and on many skills that are not necessarily used in other kinds of learning. Spanish classes may differ from other classes in a variety of ways. For instance, lectures generally play only a small role in the language classroom. Because the goal is to learn to communicate, students interact with each other and with their teacher as they learn to express themselves about things they like to do (and things they don't), their personalities, the world around them, foods, celebrations, pastimes, technology, and much more. Rather than primarily listening to the teacher, reading the text, and memorizing information as they might in a social studies class, language learners will share ideas; discuss similarities and differences between cultures; ask and answer questions; and work with others to practice new words, sounds, and sentence structures. As in Level A, your child will be given a variety of tasks to do in preparation for such an interactive class. He or she will complete written activities, perform listening tasks, watch and listen to videos, and go on the Internet. In addition, to help solidify command of words and structures, time will need to be spent on learning vocabulary and practicing the language until it starts to become second nature. Many students will find that using flash cards and doing written practice will help them become confident using the building blocks of language.

To help you help your child in this endeavor, we offer the following insights into the textbook program your child will be using, along with suggestions for ways that you can help build your child's motivation and confidence—and as a result, success in learning Spanish.

## Textbook Organization

Your child is learning Spanish using *REALIDADES*, which means "realities." The emphasis throughout the text is on learning to use the language in authentic, real ways. Chapters are organized by themes such as food and health, family and celebrations, stores and shopping, etc. Each chapter begins with a section called **A primera vista** (*At First Glance*), which gives an initial presentation of new grammar and vocabulary in the form of pictures, short dialogues, audio recordings, and video. Once students have been exposed to the new language, the **Manos a la obra** (*Let's Get to Work*) section offers lots of practice with the language as well as explanations of how the language works. The third section, **¡Adelante!** (*Moving Ahead!*), provides activities for your child to use the language by understanding readings, giving oral or written presentations, and learning more about the cultural perspectives of Spanish speakers. Finally, all chapters conclude with an at-a-glance review of the chapter material called **Repaso del capítulo** (*Chapter Review*), with summary lists and charts, and practice activities like those on the chapter test. If students have trouble with a given task, the **Repaso del capítulo** tells them where in the chapter they can go to review.

## Organization of this Workbook

The Guided Practice Activities workbook is designed to be consistent and easy to use. Each chapter consists of three main sections: vocabulary flash cards; vocabulary check sheets; and numbered worksheets to support the grammar, reading task, and oral or written presentation in the chapter.

The vocabulary flash cards review all the vocabulary words listed in the **Repaso del capítulo** (*Chapter Review*) of *REALIDADES*, Level B. On the picture cards, students write the Spanish vocabulary word in the space provided. On the cards with a printed word or phrase, students copy that Spanish word or phrase in the space provided to practice spelling.

The vocabulary checks are pages designed to be torn out of the workbook for reviewing chapter vocabulary. Students write in Spanish words or their English equivalents and then fold the paper as marked to check their answers.

Finally, the grammar tutorial sheets, which are numbered from 1 to 6, give your child more structured practice than the textbook. The first four activities provide step-by-step review and practice of the main grammar topics in the chapter. The final two activities in each chapter support the reading task and the oral presentation (in the A chapters) and writing presentation (in the B chapters) in the **¡Adelante!** sections of the textbook by focusing students on the steps required to complete the task.

## Strategies for Supporting Language Learners

Here are some suggestions that will help your child become a successful language learner.

*Routine:*

- Provide a special, quiet place for study, equipped with a Spanish-English dictionary, pens or pencils, paper, computer, and any other items your child's teacher suggests.
- Encourage your child to study Spanish at a regular time every day. A study routine will greatly facilitate the learning process.

*Strategy:*

- Remind your child that class participation and memorization are very important in a foreign language course.
- Tell your child that in reading or listening activities, as well as in the classroom, it is not necessary to understand every word. Suggest that he or she listen or look for key words to get the gist of what's being communicated.
- Encourage your child to ask questions in class if he or she is confused. Remind the child that other students may have the same question. This will minimize frustration and help your child succeed.

*Real-life connection:*

- Outside of the regular study time, encourage your child to review new words in their proper context as they relate to the chapter themes. For example, when studying the vocabulary for the household chapter, *Capítulo 6B*, have your child help with household chores and ask him or her to name the tasks in Spanish. You could also have your child label household objects with adhesive notes containing the Spanish words. Similarly, while reviewing vocabulary in section 4 of *Para empezar*, have your child bring flash cards for place names on a trip into town and review words for the buildings you pass along the way. If your child can include multiple senses while studying (see the school and say *escuela,* or taste ice cream and say *helado),* it will help reinforce study and will aid in vocabulary retention.

- Motivate your child with praise for small jobs well done, not just for big exams and final grades. A memorized vocabulary list is something to be proud of!

## Resources:

- Offer to help frequently! Your child may have great ideas for how you can facilitate his or her learning experience.
- Ask your child's teacher, or encourage your child to ask, about how to best prepare for and what to expect on tests and quizzes.
- Ask your child's teacher about the availability of audio recordings and videos that support the text. The more your child sees and hears the language, the greater the retention. There are also on-line and CD-ROM based versions of the textbook that may be useful for your child.
- Visit www.PHSchool.com with your child for more helpful tips and practice opportunities, including downloadable audio files that your child can play at home to practice Spanish. Enter the appropriate Web Code from the list on the next page for the section of the chapter that the class is working on and you will see a menu that lists the available audio files. They can be listened to on a computer or on a personal audio player.

| Capítulo | A primera vista | Manos a la obra | Repaso |
|---|---|---|---|
| **Level A** | | | |
| Para empezar | | | jcd-0099 |
| Capítulo 1A | jcd-0187 | jcd-0188 | jcd-0189 |
| Capítulo 1B | jcd-0197 | jcd-0198 | jcd-0199 |
| Capítulo 2A | jcd-0287 | jcd-0299 | jcd-0289 |
| Capítulo 2B | jcd-0297 | jcd-0298 | jcd-0299 |
| Capítulo 3A | jcd-0387 | jcd-0388 | jcd-0389 |
| Capítulo 3B | jcd-0397 | jcd-0398 | jcd-0399 |
| Capítulo 4A | jcd-0487 | jcd-0488 | jcd-0489 |
| Capítulo 4B | jcd-0497 | jcd-0498 | jcd-0499 |
| **Level B** | | | |
| Capítulo 5A | jcd-0587 | jcd-0588 | jcd-0589 |
| Capítulo 5B | jcd-0597 | jcd-0598 | jcd-0599 |
| Capítulo 6A | jcd-0687 | jcd-0688 | jcd-0689 |
| Capítulo 6B | jcd-0697 | jcd-0698 | jcd-0699 |
| Capítulo 7A | jcd-0787 | jcd-0788 | jcd-0789 |
| Capítulo 7B | jcd-0797 | jcd-0798 | jcd-0799 |
| Capítulo 8A | jcd-0887 | jcd-0888 | jcd-0889 |
| Capítulo 8B | jcd-0897 | jcd-0898 | jcd-0899 |
| Capítulo 9A | jcd-0987 | jcd-0988 | jcd-0989 |
| Capítulo 9B | jcd-0997 | jcd-0998 | jcd-0999 |

*Review:*

- Encourage your child to review previously learned material frequently, and not just before a test. Remember, learning a language is a building process, and it is important to keep using what you've already learned.
- To aid vocabulary memorization, suggest that your child try several different methods, such as saying words aloud while looking at a picture of the items, writing the words, acting them out while saying them, and so on.
- Suggest that your child organize new material using charts, graphs, pictures with labels, or other visuals that can be posted in the study area. A daily review of those visuals will help keep the material fresh.
- Help your child drill new vocabulary and grammar by using the charts and lists in the **Manos a la obra** and **Repaso del capítulo** sections.

Above all, help your child understand that a language is not acquired overnight. Just as for a first language, there is a gradual process for learning a second one. It takes time and patience, and it is important to know that mistakes are a completely natural part of the process. Remind your child that it took years to become proficient in his or her first language, and that the second one will also take time. Praise your child for even small progress in the ability to communicate in Spanish, and provide opportunities for your child to hear and use the language.

## Strategies for Using this Book

At the beginning of a new school year, it is essential to review and practice material regularly so that students do not become frustrated that they have forgotten everything. It is natural to forget, and the best way to get back on track is by frequent review. The activities in this workbook are designed to review and practice material from the *REALIDADES* textbook and to help students throughout the year.

Here are some tips for helping your child in studying Spanish this year.

*Learning vocabulary with flash cards:*

Flash cards are a useful tool for learning or reviewing vocabulary. Help your child set up a system for filing material for easy access when reviewing vocabulary, so that he or she can study independently and achieve success. A small box or index card holder can serve as a convenient storage place for the cards. You can stress the importance of organizing words by chapter to keep your child's system coordinated with the textbook.

Your child may want to use the flash card activities in this workbook as models for making his or her own flash cards. If your child is artistic, you can encourage him or her to draw the visualized words as they are done in the Guided Practice Activities workbook, writing the Spanish word on back of the card instead of below the drawing.

Flash cards are also a useful tool for you to help your child to review vocabulary. You can spend just a few minutes a day going through a handful of cards with your child. If your child has flash cards from Level A, you can use this as an opportunity to prepare for the Level B. If your child does not have his or her own flash cards, you may want to encourage him or her to work with a friend.

*Supporting reading strategies:*

The *REALIDADES* program provides students with various reading strategies that help them manage what can be a difficult task for some students. Here are some strategies that your child can use in the reading activities of the Guided Practice Activities workbook.

- **Using cognates.** When your child has difficulty with a reading at home, encourage him or her to look for words that are similar to English words in order to help decipher the meaning of the text.

- **Finding meaning using context clues.** If your child stumbles on a word or two in a reading, encourage him or her to use what is written around the word or words to find its meaning. Remind your child that it is not always necessary to know all of the words to understand the meaning of the passage.

- **Using format to find meaning.** Sometimes the title and format of a reading provide a basis for finding meaning in a reading. For example, on pages 240–241 of the Level B textbook, there is a reading about a trip to Peru. By looking at the format of that reading and the pictures, your child should be able to tell that it is a journal and that the person writes each time she is at a different location.

- **Using prior experience.** Often your child's real-life experience can help provide meaning. For example, if your child enjoys shopping and is familiar with the language used in that setting, then the theme **De compras** (*shopping*) will be a familiar setting from which to derive meaning.

### *Preparing for presentations:*

Another way to help your child use this Guided Practice Activities workbook is by helping him or her prepare for the oral and written presentations. Of course, the best way to succeed at both is by frequent practice, but here are some pointers to help your child feel more prepared for doing a presentation.

- **Using note cards.** Your child may be allowed to refer to notes when doing an oral presentation, so it is important to have neatly prepared cards. Note cards provide a good way of organizing thoughts before an entire presentation is completed, especially in the case of writing where details tend to be more specific.

- **Using graphic organizers.** Several types of graphic organizers are helpful preparation tools for presentations. Word webs are often used in your child's textbook to organize thoughts and details before a presentation. The textbook often suggests using graphic organizers as a strategy to complete he prewrite step of the writing presentation.

- **Acting it out.** With oral presentations, it is always best to run through the presentation beforehand, so that your child knows what he or she will sound like, and how long the presentation will be.

Don't hesitate to ask your child's teacher for ideas. You will find the teacher eager to help you. You may also be able to help the teacher understand special needs that your child may have, and work together with him or her to find the best techniques for helping your child learn.

Learning to speak another language is one of the most gratifying experiences a person can have. We know that your child will benefit from the effort, and will acquire a skill that will serve to enrich his or her life.

# Guided Practice Activities, Level B

This page intentionally left blank.

**Realidades** Ⓑ

**Capítulo 5A**

Nombre _____

Hora _____

Fecha _____

**Vocabulary Flash Cards, Sheet 1**

Write the Spanish vocabulary word below each picture. If there is a word or phrase, copy it in the space provided. Be sure to include the article for each noun.

| | | |
|---|---|---|
| _____ _____ | _____ _____ | _____ _____ |
| _____ _____ | _____ _____ | _____ _____ |
| _____ _____ | _____ _____ | _____ _____ |

_____

_____

_____

_____

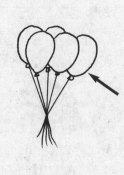

_____

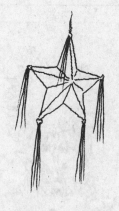

_____

_____

_____

_____

**Realidades** **B**

**Capítulo 5A**

Nombre _____

Hora _____

Fecha _____

**Vocabulary Flash Cards, Sheet 3**

el cumpleaños

el esposo

la esposa

_____

_____

_____

_____

_____

_____

_____

_____

_____

_____

_____

_____

**Realidades** **B**

**Capítulo 5A**

Nombre _____

Hora _____

Fecha _____

**Vocabulary Flash Cards, Sheet 4**

_____

_____


_____

_____


_____

_____


**el hermanastro**

**la hermanastra**

**los hijos**

_____

_____


_____

_____


_____

_____


**el hijo**

**la hija**

**el padrastro**

_____

_____


_____

_____


_____

_____

Nombre _____    Hora _____

Fecha _____    **Vocabulary Flash Cards, Sheet 5**

**la madrastra**

_____

_____

_____

_____

_____

_____

_____

_____

_____

_____

**¡Feliz cumpleaños!**

_____

_____

**celebrar**

_____

**Realidades** **B**

**Capítulo 5A**

Nombre _____

Hora _____

Fecha _____

**Vocabulary Flash Cards, Sheet 6**

| | | |
|---|---|---|
| **el video** <br><br> _____ <br> _____ | **preparar** <br><br><br> _____ | **sacar fotos** <br><br><br> _____ |
| **la foto** <br><br> _____ <br> _____ | **que** <br><br><br> _____ | **sólo** <br><br><br> _____ |
| **mayor, mayores** <br><br><br> _____ | **menor, menores** <br><br><br> _____ | **la persona** <br><br><br> _____ |

Nombre _____    Hora _____

Fecha _____    **Vocabulary Check, Sheet 1**

Tear out this page. Write the English words on the lines. Fold the paper along the dotted line to see the correct answers so you can check your work.

el abuelo          _____

la abuela          _____

el hermano         _____

la hermana         _____

el hijo            _____

la hija            _____

el padre (papá)    _____

la madre (mamá)    _____

el primo           _____

la prima           _____

el tío             _____

la tía             _____

la persona         _____

el gato            _____

el perro           _____

Fold In

Tear out this page. Write the Spanish words on the lines. Fold the paper along the dotted line to see the correct answers so you can check your work.

grandfather          _____

grandmother          _____

brother              _____

sister               _____

son                  _____

daughter             _____

father               _____

mother               _____

cousin (*male*)      _____

cousin (*female*)    _____

uncle                _____

aunt                 _____

person               _____

cat                  _____

dog                  _____

Fold In

**Realidades B**

**Capítulo 5A**

Nombre _____

Hora _____

Fecha _____

**Vocabulary Check, Sheet 3**

Tear out this page. Write the English words on the lines. Fold the paper along the dotted line to see the correct answers so you can check your work.

abrir _____

celebrar _____

decorar _____

hacer un video _____

romper _____

sacar fotos _____

la cámara _____

¡Feliz cumpleaños! _____

_____

los dulces _____

la flor, *pl.* las flores _____

el globo _____

la luz, *pl.* las luces _____

el papel picado _____

_____

el pastel _____

el regalo _____

Fold In

Tear out this page. Write the Spanish words on the lines. Fold the paper along the dotted line to see the correct answers so you can check your work.

to open _____

to celebrate _____

to decorate _____

to videotape _____

to break _____

to take pictures _____

camera _____

Happy birthday! _____

_____

candy _____

flower _____

balloon _____

light _____

cut-paper decorations _____

cake _____

gift, present _____

To hear a complete list of the vocabulary for this chapter, go to Disc 2, Track 1 on the Guided Practice Audio CD, or go to www.phschool.com and type in the Web Code jcd-0589. Then click on **Repaso del capítulo.**

Fold In

# The verb *tener* (p. 42)

- You have already learned some forms of the verb **tener** (*to have*): **tengo, tienes.**
- **Tener** is an irregular verb. Here are its forms.

| yo | **tengo** | nosotros/nosotras | **tenemos** |
|---|---|---|---|
| tú | **tienes** | vosotros/vosotras | **tenéis** |
| usted/él/ella | **tiene** | ustedes/ellos/ellas | **tienen** |

**A.** Write the correct form of **tener** next to each subject pronoun.

1. él _____
2. usted _____
3. ellos _____
4. nosotras _____
5. yo _____
6. tú _____

- **Tener** is used to show relationship or possession.
  - **Tengo** dos hermanas.          *I have two sisters.*
  - **Tienes** una bicicleta.          *You have a bicycle.*

- **Tener** is also used to express age, hunger, and thirst.
  - **Tengo** catorce años.          *I am fourteen years old.*
  - **Tengo** hambre.          *I am hungry.*
  - **Tengo** sed.          *I am thirsty.*

**B.** Read each numbered sentence with **tener**. Then write the number of that sentence in the correct column in the chart, depending on whether **tener** is used to express possession, age, thirst/hunger, or relationship. Follow the model.

| possession | age | thirst/hunger | relationship |
|---|---|---|---|
|  | *#1* |  |  |

1. ¿Cuántos años tiene tu tío?
2. Nosotras tenemos diez primos.
3. ¿Tiene sed tu padre?
4. Mi hermana tiene tres años.
5. Yo tengo un regalo para mi abuela.
6. Mis primos tienen mucha hambre.

**C.** Now, look at the following sentences and write in the missing forms of **tener**.

1. Mi prima Ana _____ once años.
2. Yo _____ un regalo para mi tía.
3. Mis hermanos _____ mucha hambre.
4. Nosotros _____ tres gatos.
5. ¿Cuántos años _____ tu padre?
6. ¿ _____ sed tu hermano?

**Go Online** WEB CODE jcd-0504
PHSchool.com

**Realidades B**

**Capítulo 5A**

Nombre _____

Fecha _____

Hora _____

**Guided Practice Activities 5A-2**

# The verb *tener (continued)*

**D.** Look at the family tree. Write forms of **tener** to complete each sentence below it.

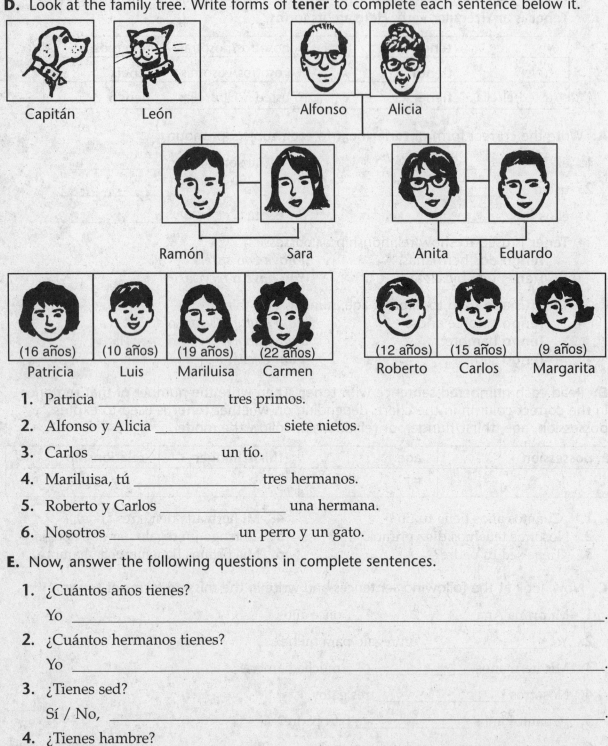

Capitán    León    Alfonso    Alicia

Ramón    Sara    Anita    Eduardo

(16 años)    (10 años)    (19 años)    (22 años)    (12 años)    (15 años)    (9 años)
Patricia    Luis    Mariluisa    Carmen    Roberto    Carlos    Margarita

1. Patricia _____ tres primos.

2. Alfonso y Alicia _____ siete nietos.

3. Carlos _____ un tío.

4. Mariluisa, tú _____ tres hermanos.

5. Roberto y Carlos _____ una hermana.

6. Nosotros _____ un perro y un gato.

**E.** Now, answer the following questions in complete sentences.

1. ¿Cuántos años tienes?

   Yo _____.

2. ¿Cuántos hermanos tienes?

   Yo _____.

3. ¿Tienes sed?

   Sí / No, _____.

4. ¿Tienes hambre?

   Sí / No, _____.

Go Online   WEB CODE jcd-0504
PHSchool.com

# Possessive adjectives (p. 48)

- Possessive adjectives are used to indicate who owns what and to show relationships.

- In English, *my, your, his, her, our,* and *their* are possessive adjectives.

| yo | **mi/mis** | nosotros<br>nosotras | **nuestro/nuestros**<br>**nuestra/nuestras** |
|---|---|---|---|
| tú | **tu/tus** | vosotros<br>vosotras | **vuestro/vuestros**<br>**vuestra/vuestras** |
| usted/él/ella | **su/sus** | ustedes/ellos/ellas | **su/sus** |

- Spanish possessive adjectives, just like other adjectives, change their endings to reflect number. The **nosotros** and **nosotras** forms (**nuestro, nuestra, nuestros, nuestras**) also change to reflect gender.

**mi** herman**o** / **mis** herman**os**           BUT:
**mi** hija / **mis** hijas                    nuestr**o** tío / nuestr**os** tíos
**tu** flor / **tus** flor**es**                  nuestr**a** tía / nuestr**as** tías

**A.** Look at each noun. Write **S** if the noun is singular and **P** if it is plural.

1. _____ primo            5. _____ pastel

2. _____ regalos          6. _____ tío

3. _____ hijas            7. _____ globos

4. _____ flor             8. _____ familias

**B.** Now, circle the correct possessive adjective for each of the nouns from **part A**.

1. ( **mi** / **mis** ) primo      5. ( **tu** / **tus** ) pastel

2. ( **su** / **sus** ) regalos    6. ( **mi** / **mis** ) tío

3. ( **tu** / **tus** ) hijas      7. ( **su** / **sus** ) globos

4. ( **mi** / **mis** ) flor       8. ( **tu** / **tus** ) familias

**C.** Write **mi** in front of each singular noun and **mis** in front of each plural noun.

1. _____ piñata

2. _____ hermanos

3. _____ regalos

4. _____ flores

**Realidades B**

**Capítulo 5A**

Nombre _____

Hora _____

Fecha _____

**Guided Practice Activities 5A-4**

## Possessive adjectives *(continued)*

**D.** Look at each noun. Circle **S** if it is singular and **P** if it is plural. Circle **M** if it is masculine and **F** if it is feminine. Follow the model.

Modelo    pasteles        ( S /(P)) and ((M)/ F )

1. decoraciones  ( S / P ) and ( M / F )   4. flores  ( S / P ) and ( M / F )
2. hijos  ( S / P ) and ( M / F )   5. luz  ( S / P ) and ( M / F )
3. gato  ( S / P ) and ( M / F )   6. globos  ( S / P ) and ( M / F )

**E.** Below are the nouns from **part D**. Write **nuestro, nuestra, nuestros,** or **nuestras** in front of each one. Follow the model.

Modelo    _nuestros_ pasteles

1. _____ decoraciones   4. _____ flores
2. _____ hijos   5. _____ luz
3. _____ gato   6. _____ globos

**F.** Circle the correct word to complete each sentence.

1. Tenemos ( **nuestros / nuestras** ) decoraciones en el coche.
2. Voy a la fiesta con ( **mi / mis** ) abuelos.
3. Aquí tienes ( **tu / tus** ) regalo.
4. Alicia va a hacer una piñata con ( **su / sus** ) hermano.
5. ( **Nuestro / Nuestra** ) familia saca muchas fotos en las fiestas.
6. Ella va a la fiesta con ( **su / sus** ) perro.

**G.** Write the correct form of the possessive adjective indicated to complete each sentence. Follow the models.

Modelos  nuestro: Ella es _nuestra_ tía.
  mi:  Roberto y Luis son _mis_ primos.

1. tu:  Elena y Margarita son _____ hermanas.
2. mi:  León es _____ perro.
3. nuestro:  Ellos son _____ primos.
4. su:  Adela es _____ abuela.
5. su:  Adela y Hernando son _____ abuelos.
6. nuestro:  Roberto es _____ hijo.
7. nuestro:  Lidia y Susana son _____ tías.

Go Online WEB CODE jcd-0505 PHSchool.com

**Realidades** **B**

**Capítulo 5A**

Nombre _____

Fecha _____

Hora _____

**Guided Practice Activities 5A-5**

## Lectura: ¡Te invitamos a nuestra miniteca! (pp. 54–55)

**A.** Part of the reading in your textbook is an invitation to a special celebration. Before skimming the reading, write four pieces of information you would expect to find on an invitation to such a party.

1. _____

2. _____

3. _____

4. _____

> *Felipe Rivera López*
> *y Guadalupe Treviño Ibarra*
> *esperan el honor de su asistencia*
> *el sábado, 15 de mayo de 2004*
> *para celebrar los quince años de su hija*
> *María Teresa Rivera Treviño.*

**B.** Read through the text of the first part of the invitation (top right). Complete the following.

1. Circle the day of the week in the paragraph above.

2. Underline the date of the party.

3. What is the daughter's full name? _____

_____

> *Misa*
> *a las cuatro de la tarde*
> *Iglesia Nuestra Señora de Guadalupe*
> *2374 Avenida Linda Vista, San Diego, California*
> *Recepción y cena-baile a las seis de la tarde*
> *Restaurante Luna*
> *7373 Calle Florida, San Diego, California*

**C.** Now, read the second part of the invitation and answer the questions below.

1. Write the times that each of the following takes place:

   **(a)** the Mass _____     **(b)** the reception _____

2. What will people be doing at the reception? _____

3. At what kind of place will the reception be held? _____

**D.** Now look back at **part A**. Did you find all of the information you were looking for in the reading? Fill in the simple facts of the reception below.

For whom: _____

Time: _____

Date: _____

Location: _____

WEB CODE jcd-0506

**Realidades B**

**Capítulo 5A**

Nombre _____

Hora _____

Fecha _____

**Guided Practice Activities 5A-6**

## Presentación oral (p. 57) *Answers will vary.*

**Task:** Pretend you are living with a host family in Chile. They want to know about your family back home. Show them photographs of two family members and talk about the people shown.

**A.** You will need to have brought in two family photos or "created" photos from an imaginary family by using pictures from a magazine. Use the chart below to organize what you want to say about each person. Follow the model and write similar information about your family members.

| Nombre | Es mi... | Edad | Actividad favorita |
|--------|----------|------|--------------------|
| Isabel | hermana menor | 9 años | le gusta cantar |
|  |  |  |  |
|  |  |  |  |

**B.** Since you will be presenting the information above orally, you will need to put everything into complete sentences. Read the model below to get you started. Be sure to practice speaking clearly when you read the model.

> *Se llama Isabel. Ella es mi hermana menor. Tiene nueve años. A Isabel le gusta cantar. Es muy artística.*

**C.** Fill in the spaces below with the information you gathered from **part A**. Make sure you provide all the information you listed about each person.

**Person 1:** Se llama _____. ( **Él / Ella** ) es mi _____.

Tiene _____ años. A _____ le gusta _____.

Es _____.

**Person 2:** Se llama _____. ( **Él / Ella** ) es mi _____.

Tiene _____ años. A _____ le gusta _____.

Es _____.

**D.** Practice your presentation with the photos. Remember to:

_____ provide all the information on each family member

_____ use complete sentences

_____ speak clearly

**Realidades** **B**

**Capítulo 5B**

Nombre _____

Hora _____

Fecha _____

**Vocabulary Flash Cards, Sheet 1**

Write the Spanish vocabulary word below each picture. If there is a word or phrase, copy it in the space provided. Be sure to include the article for each noun.

El desayuno El almuerzo

_____

_____

_____

_____

6'5"

_____

SUGAR

_____

_____

5'0"

_____

_____

_____

Nombre _____

Hora _____

Fecha _____

**Vocabulary Flash Cards, Sheet 2**

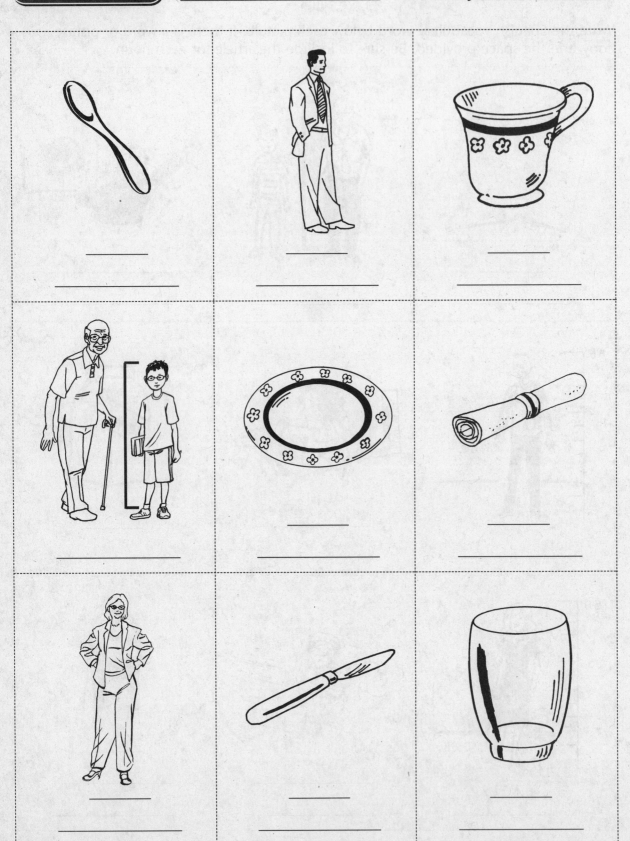

_____

_____

_____

_____

_____

_____

_____

_____

_____

**Realidades B**

**Capítulo 5B**

Nombre _____

Hora _____

Fecha _____

**Vocabulary Flash Cards, Sheet 3**

traer

el plato
principal

**Realidades** **B**

**Capítulo 5B**

Nombre _____

Hora _____

Fecha _____

**Vocabulary Flash Cards, Sheet 4**

corto,
corta

_____ ,

_____

guapo,
guapa

_____ ,

_____

el joven

_____

_____

la joven

_____

_____

el pelo

_____

_____

canoso

_____

_____

castaño

_____

negro

_____

rubio

_____

**Realidades B**

**Capítulo 5B**

Nombre _____

Hora _____

Fecha _____

**Vocabulary Flash Cards, Sheet 5**

**pelirrojo,
pelirroja**

_____ ,

_____

**delicioso,
deliciosa**

_____ ,

_____

**desear**

_____

**pedir**

_____

**rico,
rica**

_____ ,

_____

**Me falta(n)...**

_____

_____

**Quisiera...**

_____

**ahora**

_____

**¿Algo
más?**

_____

_____

**Realidades** **B**

**Capítulo 5B**

Nombre _____

Fecha _____

Hora _____

**Vocabulary Flash Cards, Sheet 6**

De nada.

_____

_____

otro,
otra

_____,

_____

¿Me trae...?

_____

_____

Le traigo...

_____

¡Qué!

_____

largo,
larga

_____

_____

yo
traigo

_____

el joven

_____

de postre

_____

**Realidades B**

**Capítulo 5B**

Nombre _____

Hora _____

Fecha _____

**Vocabulary Check, Sheet 1**

Tear out this page. Write the English words on the lines. Fold the paper along the dotted line to see the correct answers so you can check your work.

el hombre                  _____

la mujer                   _____

corto, corta               _____

joven                      _____

largo, larga               _____

viejo, vieja               _____

el pelo                    _____

canoso                     _____

castaño                    _____

negro                      _____

rubio                      _____

pelirrojo,                 _____
pelirroja

desear                     _____

pedir                      _____

el plato                   _____
principal                  _____

Fold In

Tear out this page. Write the Spanish words on the lines. Fold the paper along the dotted line to see the correct answers so you can check your work.

man _____

woman _____

short (length) _____

young _____

long _____

old _____

hair _____

gray _____

brown (chestnut) _____

black _____

blond _____

red-haired _____

_____

to want _____

to order _____

main dish _____

_____

Fold In

Tear out this page. Write the English words on the lines. Fold the paper along the dotted line to see the correct answers so you can check your work.

el postre _____

rico, rica _____

el azúcar _____

la cuchara _____

el cuchillo _____

la pimienta _____

el plato _____

la sal _____

la servilleta _____

la taza _____

el tenedor _____

el vaso _____

el camarero _____

la camarera _____

la cuenta _____

el menú _____

Fold In

Tear out this page. Write the Spanish words on the lines. Fold the paper along the dotted line to see the correct answers so you can check your work.

dessert _____

rich, tasty _____

sugar _____

spoon _____

knife _____

pepper _____

plate, dish _____

salt _____

napkin _____

cup _____

fork _____

glass _____

waiter _____

waitress _____

bill _____

menu _____

Fold In

To hear a complete list of the vocabulary for this chapter, go to Disc 2, Track 2 on the Guided Practice Audio CD, or go to www.phschool.com and type in the Web Code jcd-0599. Then click on **Repaso del capítulo.**

# The verb *venir* (p. 76)

- The forms of **venir** are similar to the forms of **tener** that you just learned. Notice that the **yo** forms of both verbs end in **-go**.

| yo | **vengo** | nosotros/nosotras | **venimos** |
|---|---|---|---|
| tú | **vienes** | vosotros/vosotras | **venís** |
| usted/él/ella | **viene** | ustedes/ellos/ellas | **vienen** |

**A.** Circle all the forms of **venir** you see in this conversation.

RAÚL: ¿Vienes a la fiesta?

ANA: Sí, vengo a las ocho y media.

Mis padres vienen también.

RAÚL: Muy bien. Mis amigos no vienen, pero mi hermano sí viene.

ANA: ¿Cuándo vienen?

RAÚL: Venimos a las nueve.

**B.** Now, write the forms of **venir** that you circled in **part A** in the correct row of the table. Write only one form of **venir** for each subject pronoun. The first one has been done for you.

| Subject pronoun | Form of *venir* |
|---|---|
| 1. yo | |
| 2. tú | *Vienes* |
| 3. usted/él/ella | |
| 4. nosotros | |
| 5. ustedes/ellos/ellas | |

**C.** Complete the following conversation by circling the correct forms of **venir**.

ISABEL: ¿( **Vienes** / **Vienen** ) ustedes a la fiesta?

MÍA: Sí, Marcos y yo ( **vienen** / **venimos** ). Pero Luis no ( **vienes** / **viene** ).

ISABEL: ¿Por qué no ( **viene** / **vengo** ) Luis?

MÍA: Tiene que trabajar. ¿ ( **Venimos** / **Vienes** ) tú?

ISABEL: Sí. ( **Vengo** / **Vienen** ) a las ocho.

MÍA: ¡Qué bien! Nosotros ( **venimos** / **vienes** ) a las ocho también.

- **Venir** is used to say that someone is coming to a place or an event.

**D.** Write forms of **venir** to say when people are coming to the party.

1. Nosotras _____ a las ocho y cuarto.

2. Tú _____ a las nueve menos cuarto.

3. Elena y Olga _____ a las nueve y media.

4. Yo _____ a las ocho.

5. Marcos _____ a las diez y cuarto.

6. Usted _____ a las diez menos cuarto.

7. Ustedes _____ a las diez.

**E.** This agenda shows when people have appointments. Complete each sentence to say when each person is coming. Follow the model.

| Modelo | _La Sra. Ramos viene_ a las ocho y media. |

8:00
8:30 La Sra. Ramos
9:00 Marta
10:00 Raúl y Josefina
10:45 Yo
11:00
11:30 tú
12:00 Carmen y yo
Pedro
1:00
2:00
2:30 Roberto y tú
3:00
3:30 Lucía y Ramón
4:00
5:00

1. _____ a las nueve.

2. _____ a las diez.

3. _____ a las once menos cuarto.

4. _____ a las once y media.

5. _____ a las doce.

6. _____ a la una.

7. _____ a las dos y media.

8. _____ a las tres y media.

**F.** Answer each question by completing the sentences. Follow the model.

| Modelo | ¿A qué hora vienes a la clase de español? |
| | Yo _vengo_ a la clase de español _a las diez y media_ . |

1. ¿A qué hora vienes a la escuela?

   Yo _____ a la escuela _____.

2. ¿A qué hora vienes a la clase de español?

   Yo _____ a la clase de español _____.

3. ¿A qué hora vienes a casa?

   Yo _____ a casa _____.

**Go Online** WEB CODE jcd-0513
PHSchool.com

**Realidades** **B**

**Capítulo 5B**

Nombre _____

Hora _____

Fecha _____

**Guided Practice Activities 5B-3**

## The verbs *ser* and *estar* (p. 78)

- There are two Spanish verbs that mean "to be": **ser** and **estar**.
- Review their forms in the present tense.

| ser | | | |
|---|---|---|---|
| yo | **soy** | nosotros/nosotras | **somos** |
| tú | **eres** | vosotros/vosotras | **sois** |
| usted/él/ella | **es** | ustedes/ellos/ellas | **son** |

| estar | | | |
|---|---|---|---|
| yo | **estoy** | nosotros/nosotras | **estamos** |
| tú | **estás** | vosotros/vosotras | **estáis** |
| usted/él/ella | **está** | ustedes/ellos/ellas | **están** |

**A.** Circle the form of **ser** or **estar** that is used in each sentence.

1. Mi madre es profesora.
2. Ellas son de México.
3. Las decoraciones están en mi casa.
4. Nosotras somos artísticas.
5. Yo estoy enferma.
6. Los libros están en la mesa.
7. Tú estás en la oficina.
8. Yo soy la prima de Ana.

**B.** Look at the forms of **ser** and **estar** that you circled in **part A**. Decide why **ser** or **estar** was used in each. Write the reason using the chart in the explanation on page 258 in your textbook to find the reason why **ser** or **estar** was used in each sentence. Write each reason in the right-hand side of the chart. The first one has been done for you.

| Forms of *ser* and *estar* | Reason |
|---|---|
| 1. *es* | *who a person is* |
| 2. | |
| 3. | |
| 4. | |
| 5. | |
| 6. | |
| 7. | |
| 8. | |

**Realidades B**

**Capítulo 5B**

Nombre _____

Hora _____

Fecha _____

**Guided Practice Activities 5B-4**

# The verbs *ser* and *estar* (continued)

**C.** Circle the correct form of the verb **ser** in each sentence.

1. Mis padres ( **son / somos** ) profesores.

2. Yo ( **soy / eres** ) muy atrevida.

3. La comida ( **es / eres** ) de un restaurante.

**D.** Circle the correct form of the verb **estar** in each sentence.

1. Tú ( **estoy / estás** ) muy cansado hoy.

2. La computadora ( **está / estamos** ) en la oficina.

3. Nosotros ( **estamos / están** ) muy ocupados.

**E.** Circle the correct form of **ser** or **estar** in these sentences. Look back at the chart with the uses of **ser** and **estar** if you need help.

1. Mis abuelos ( **son / están** ) profesores de matemáticas.

2. Yo ( **soy / estoy** ) enfermo hoy.

3. Tú ( **eres / estás** ) en la clase de historia.

4. Tomás ( **es / está** ) de Argentina.

5. Ustedes ( **son / están** ) argentinos también.

6. Nosotras ( **somos / estamos** ) muy cansadas.

7. Los libros ( **son / están** ) muy interesantes.

8. Los libros ( **son / están** ) en la biblioteca.

**F.** Write the correct form of **ser** or **estar** to complete each sentence.

1. Tú _____ en la oficina.

2. Nosotras _____ muy ocupadas hoy.

3. Yo _____ estudiante.

4. Mi padre _____ profesor.

5. El video _____ interesante.

6. Los videos _____ en la biblioteca.

7. Nosotros _____ de Guatemala.

8. Tú _____ muy simpático.

Go Online WEB CODE jcd-0514
PHSchool.com

**Realidades B**

**Capítulo 5B**

Nombre _____

Hora _____

Fecha _____

**Guided Practice Activities 5B-5**

## Lectura: Una visita a Santa Fe (pp. 84–85)

**A.** The reading in your textbook is about the city of Santa Fe. What kinds of information would you expect to find in such a reading? List three ideas below.

1. _____

2. _____

3. _____

**B.** As you skim the reading you will come across some new cognates. Write the English word for each Spanish cognate listed below.

1. visita _____

2. historia _____

3. museo _____

4. típica _____

5. histórico _____

6. tradicional _____

**C.** Did you find some activities when you skimmed the reading? If not, look again to find three activities that the cousins are going to do during their visit to Santa Fe. Write the three activities in Spanish below.

1. _____

2. _____

3. _____

**D.** Now, read the paragraph below from your textbook and answer the questions in English that follow.

> *Durante los días de su visita, el Rancho va a celebrar "un fandango", un baile histórico y típico, con una cena tradicional. Toda la comida es riquísima, pero nuestro plato favorito es el chile con carne y queso. Después de comer, vamos a bailar.*

1. What is a "fandango"? _____

2. What kind of meal will they have to accompany the "fandango"?

   _____

3. What is their favorite dish at the restaurant? _____

4. Which comes first, the meal or dancing? _____

**Realidades B**

**Capítulo 5B**

Nombre _____

Hora _____

Fecha _____

**Guided Practice Activities 5B-6**

# Presentación escrita (p. 87)

**Task:** Pretend your town needs a Spanish-language community guide for restaurants written. Write a review of your favorite local restaurant in Spanish.

**❶ Prewrite.** Compile the information you will need in order to write about your favorite restaurant. Fill in the information on the lines next to each category.

1. nombre _____

2. descripción general _____

_____

3. platos principales _____

4. postres _____

**❷ Draft.**

**A.** In order to prepare your first draft, write sentences with the information you compiled in **section 1 (Prewrite)**.

1. El restaurante se llama _____.

2. Es un restaurante _____ con

_____.

3. Los _____ son riquísimos.

4. Hay _____, _____ y _____ también.

**B.** Read the model below to give you an idea of what a complete review could look like.

> *Café Beló es un café tranquilo con un ambiente intelectual donde puedes pasar el tiempo en la compañía de un buen amigo o un buen libro. Los precios son baratos. Puedes comer un sándwich, una ensalada, un postre o simplemente beber un café. Los postres son riquísimos. Un "plus" es la presentación de grupos musicales los fines de semana.*

**C.** Use the sentences you wrote in **part A** above and add anything useful from the model to construct your complete review.

**❸ Revise.** Read through your review. Then you will share it with a partner. You should each check for:

_____ adjective agreement (masculine words with masculine endings, feminine words with feminine endings)

_____ correct use of verb forms

_____ correct spelling

_____ persuasiveness of your review

Write the Spanish vocabulary word below each picture. If there is a word or phrase, copy it in the space provided. Be sure to include the article for each noun.

**Realidades** (B)

**Capítulo 6A**

Nombre _____

Fecha _____

Hora _____

**Vocabulary Flash Cards, Sheet 2**

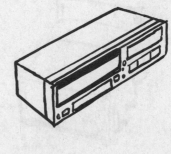

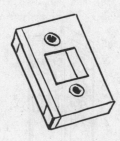

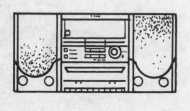

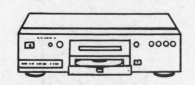

_____

_____

_____

_____

_____

_____

_____

_____

_____

**Realidades B**

**Capítulo 6A**

Nombre _____

Hora _____

Fecha _____

**Vocabulary Flash Cards, Sheet 3**

¿De qué color...?

_____ - _____

gris

_____

los colores

_____

azul

_____

marrón

_____

amarillo, amarilla

_____,

_____

blanco, blanca

_____,

_____

morado, morada

_____,

_____

**rojo,
roja**

_____,

_____

**anaranjado,
anaranjada**

_____,

_____

**importante**

_____

**rosado,
rosada**

_____,

_____

**feo,
fea**

_____,

_____

**mismo,
misma**

_____,

_____

**verde**

_____

**grande**

_____

**pequeño,
pequeña**

_____,

_____

**Realidades B**

**Capítulo 6A**

Nombre _____

Hora _____

Fecha _____

**Vocabulary Flash Cards, Sheet 5**

**propio,**
**propia**

_____ ,

_____

**el / la**
**mejor**

_____

_____

**la**
**cosa**

_____

_____

**a la**
**derecha (de)**

_____ _____

_____

**menos...**
**que**

_____

_____

**para**
**mí**

_____

_____

**a la**
**izquierda (de)**

_____ _____

_____

**el / la**
**peor**

_____

_____

**para**
**ti**

_____

_____

| | | |
|---|---|---|
| **el dormitorio** _____ _____ | **la posesión** _____ _____ | **bonito, bonita** _____ , _____ |
| **poder** _____ _____ | **los /las mejores** _____ _____ | **mejor(es) que** _____ _____ |
| **negro, negra** _____ _____ | **los / las peores** _____ _____ | **peor(es) que** _____ _____ |

Nombre _____   Hora _____

Fecha _____   **Vocabulary Check, Sheet 1**

Tear out this page. Write the English words on the lines. Fold the paper along the dotted line to see the correct answers so you can check your work.

la alfombra _____

el armario _____

la cama _____

la cómoda _____

las cortinas _____

el cuadro _____

el despertador _____

el dormitorio _____

el espejo _____

el estante _____

_____

la lámpara _____

la mesita _____

la pared _____

el equipo de sonido _____

el lector DVD _____

el televisor _____

la videocasetera _____

Fold In

Tear out this page. Write the Spanish words on the lines. Fold the paper along the dotted line to see the correct answers so you can check your work.

rug _____

closet _____

bed _____

dresser _____

curtains _____

painting _____

alarm clock _____

bedroom _____

mirror _____

shelf, bookshelf _____

lamp _____

night table _____

wall _____

sound (stereo) system _____

DVD player _____

television set _____

VCR _____

Fold In ←

**Realidades B**

**Capítulo 6A**

Nombre _____

Hora _____

Fecha _____

**Vocabulary Check, Sheet 3**

Tear out this page. Write the English words on the lines. Fold the paper along the dotted line to see the correct answers so you can check your work.

amarillo,
amarilla          _____

anaranjado,
anaranjada        _____

azul              _____

blanco, blanca    _____

gris              _____

marrón            _____

morado, morada    _____

rojo, roja        _____

rosado, rosada    _____

verde             _____

bonito, bonita    _____

feo, fea          _____

grande            _____

importante        _____

mismo, misma      _____

pequeño,
pequeña           _____

Fold In

Nombre _____  Hora _____

Fecha _____  **Vocabulary Check, Sheet 4**

Tear out this page. Write the Spanish words on the lines. Fold the paper along the dotted line to see the correct answers so you can check your work.

yellow          _____
                _____

orange          _____
                _____

blue            _____

white           _____

gray            _____

brown           _____

purple          _____

red             _____

pink            _____

green           _____

pretty          _____

ugly            _____

large           _____

important       _____

same            _____

small           _____
                _____

To hear a complete list of the vocabulary for this chapter, go to Disc 2, Track 3 on the Guided Practice Audio CD, or go to www.phschool.com and type in the Web Code jcd-0689. Then click on **Repaso del capítulo**.

Fold In

# Making comparisons (p. 106)

- Use **más** + adjective + **que** to compare two people, things, or actions:

  El libro es **más interesante que** el video.

  *The book is **more interesting than** the video.*

- Use **menos** + adjective + **que** to compare two people, things, or actions:

  Correr es **menos divertido que** montar en bicicleta.

  *Running is **less fun than** riding a bike.*

**A.** Below are six comparisons. Write a + (plus sign) next to the ones that give the idea of "greater than" or "more than." Write a – (minus sign) next to the ones that give the idea of "worse than" or "less than." Follow the models.

Modelos   más simpático que        __+__
          menos ordenada que       __–__

1. menos divertido que  _____        4. más interesante que  _____
2. más simpático que  _____          5. menos paciente que  _____
3. más reservada que  _____          6. menos atrevida que  _____

**B.** The sentences below are marked with a + (plus sign) or a – (minus sign). Write in **más** if there is a + and **menos** if there is a –.

1. + El perro es _____ simpático que el gato.
2. – Luisa es _____ artística que Beatriz.
3. – Tomás es _____ trabajador que Marcos.
4. + La bicicleta es _____ grande que el monopatín.

- Some adjectives have special forms for comparisons. See the chart below.

| Adjective | | Comparative | |
|---|---|---|---|
| bueno / buena | *good* | **mejor (que)** | *better than* |
| malo / mala | *bad* | **peor (que)** | *worse than* |
| viejo / vieja | *old* | **mayor (que)** | *older than* |
| joven | *young* | **menor (que)** | *younger than* |

**C.** Choose the correct comparative to complete each sentence.

1. Lorena tiene catorce años. Lidia tiene quince años. Lorena es ( **mayor** / **menor** ) que Lidia.

2. El restaurante grande es malo. El restaurante pequeño es bueno. El restaurante grande es ( **mejor** / **peor** ) que el restaurante pequeño.

3. Mi abuela tiene sesenta años. Tu abuela tiene cincuenta y ocho años. Mi abuela es ( **mayor** / **menor** ) que tu abuela.

**Realidades** B

**Capítulo 6A**

Nombre _____

Fecha _____

Hora _____

**Guided Practice Activities 6A-2**

# The superlative (p. 110)

- To say someone or something is the *most* or the *least*:

    **el / la / los / las** + noun + **más / menos** + adjective

    Es **el libro más interesante** de la biblioteca.

- To say someone or something is the *best* or the *worst*:

    **el / la / los / las** + **mejor(es) / peor(es)** + noun

    Es **el peor libro** de la biblioteca.

**A.** Below are eight superlative expressions. Write a + (plus sign) next to the ones that give the idea of the *most* or the *best*. Write a – (minus sign) next to the ones that give the idea of the *least* or the *worst*.

1. la lámpara más grande _____
2. la mesita más fea _____
3. el peor video _____
4. las mejores cortinas _____

5. el espejo menos feo _____
6. la alfombra menos bonita _____
7. los peores cuadros _____
8. los mejores despertadores _____

**B.** Look at each sentence and see whether it is marked with a + or a –. Write in **más** if there is a + and **menos** if there is a –.

1. + Mi tío es la persona _____ simpática de mi familia.
2. – La cama es la _____ grande de todas.
3. – Marzo es el mes _____ bonito del año.
4. + Sandra es la persona _____ divertida de la familia.

**C.** Choose the correct superlative to complete each sentence. Circle the word you have chosen.

1. Me gusta mucho nadar y montar en bicicleta. Para mí, julio es el ( **mejor** / **peor** ) mes del año.

2. Todos mis primos son inteligentes, pero Alberto es el ( **más** / **menos** ) inteligente de todos. Es muy estudioso y trabajador también.

3. Me gusta mucho esquiar. Para mí, julio es el ( **mejor** / **peor** ) mes del año.

4. No me gustan los libros aburridos. Tu libro es el ( **más** / **menos** ) aburrido de todos. Es bastante interesante.

5. Mis abuelos son muy divertidos. Son las personas ( **más** / **menos** ) divertidas de la familia.

6. No me gusta esta cama. Es la cama ( **más** / **menos** ) grande de la casa.

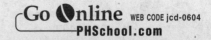

## Stem-changing verbs: *poder* and *dormir* (p. 112)

- **Poder** (*to be able to do something*) and **dormir** (*to sleep*) are both stem-changing verbs like **jugar**, which you learned previously. Just like **jugar**, only the **nosotros/nosotras** and **vosotros/vosotras** forms of **poder** and **dormir** do not change their stems.

- Here are the forms of **poder** and **dormir**:

| yo | **puedo** | nosotros/nosotras | **podemos** |
|---|---|---|---|
| tú | **puedes** | vosotros/vosotras | **podéis** |
| usted/él/ella | **puede** | ustedes/ellos/ellas | **pueden** |

| yo | **duermo** | nosotros/nosotras | **dormimos** |
|---|---|---|---|
| tú | **duermes** | vosotros/vosotras | **dormís** |
| usted/él/ella | **duerme** | ustedes/ellos/ellas | **duermen** |

**A.** Circle the forms of **poder** and **dormir** in each sentence. Then underline the stem in each verb you circled. The first one has been done for you.

1. (Dormim)os ocho horas al día.

2. ¿Puedes montar en bicicleta?

3. No puedo trabajar hoy.

4. Mis hermanos duermen mucho.

5. Podemos traer la comida.

6. Duermo mucho los fines de semana.

7. No podemos hablar francés.

8. Ud. duerme en una cama grande.

**B.** Now, write the words you circled in **part A** next to each subject pronoun below.

1. nosotros _____

2. tú _____

3. yo _____

4. ellos _____

5. nosotros _____

6. yo _____

7. nosotros _____

8. Ud. _____

**C.** Circle the correct form of **poder** or **dormir** to complete each sentence.

1. Mis amigos y yo ( **dormimos** / **duermen** ) diez horas al día.

2. Roberto no ( **puedo** / **puede** ) ir a la fiesta.

3. Ustedes ( **dormimos** / **duermen** ) en la cama más grande de la casa.

4. Tú y yo ( **puedes** / **podemos** ) traer unos discos compactos.

5. Linda y Natalia ( **duermo** / **duermen** ) en un dormitorio grande.

6. Nosotros no ( **podemos** / **puedes** ) usar el lector DVD.

7. Tú ( **dormimos** / **duermes** ) en el dormitorio con la alfombra azul.

**Realidades B**

**Capítulo 6A**

Nombre _____

Fecha _____

Hora _____

**Guided Practice Activities 6A-4**

## Stem-changing verbs: *poder* and *dormir (continued)*

**D.** Complete the sentences with forms of **poder** and **dormir**. Follow the models.

Modelos   Paco (**poder**) ir a la biblioteca.

Paco ___*puede*___ ir a la biblioteca.

Mónica (**dormir**) en el dormitorio grande.

Mónica ___*duerme*___ en el dormitorio grande.

1.  Olivia (**poder**) montar en monopatín.

    Olivia _____ montar en monopatín.

2.  Javier (**dormir**) ocho horas al día.

    Javier _____ ocho horas al día.

3.  Tú (**dormir**) en un dormitorio con tu hermano.

    Tú _____ en un dormitorio con tu hermano.

4.  Yo (**poder**) usar la videocasetera.

    Yo _____ usar la videocasetera.

5.  Nosotros (**poder**) comprar unas cortinas para el dormitorio.

    Nosotros _____ comprar unas cortinas para el dormitorio.

6.  Nosotros (**dormir**) en un dormitorio pequeño.

    Nosotros _____ en un dormitorio pequeño.

7.  Ustedes (**dormir**) mucho los fines de semana.

    Ustedes _____ mucho los fines de semana.

**E.** Write sentences about yourself and your friends using forms of **poder**. Follow the models. Use ideas from the list or other words you know.

> montar en bicicleta / esquiar / patinar / montar en monopatín /
> hablar español / nadar / patinar / tocar la guitarra / jugar a ¿...?

Modelos   Yo ___*puedo montar en bicicleta*___ .

Mis amigos y yo ___*podemos nadar*___ .

1.  Yo _____ .

2.  Yo no _____ .

3.  Mis amigos y yo _____ .

4.  Mis amigos y yo no _____ .

**Realidades B**

**Capítulo 6A**

Nombre _____

Fecha _____

Hora _____

**Guided Practice Activities 6A-5**

## Lectura: El desastre en mi dormitorio (pp. 116–117)

**A.** Try to guess the meaning of the following cognates. If you are having difficulty, skim through the reading in your textbook to find these words in context. Write your answers in the spaces below.

1. desastre _____
2. posesiones _____
3. desorden _____

4. situación _____
5. recomendar _____
6. considerar _____

**B.** The statements below refer to one of the roommates from the reading in your textbook. The roommates' names are Rosario and Marta. After each statement, circle **M** if it describes **Marta** or **R** if it describes **Rosario**.

1. **M R** Le gusta el orden.
2. **M R** Le gusta el desorden.
3. **M R** Su color favorito es el negro.

4. **M R** Su color favorito es el amarillo.
5. **M R** Hay comida en el suelo.
6. **M R** Hay postre en el escritorio.

**C.** The second part of the reading in your textbook is the response from the advice columnist, Magdalena, to Marta's letter. Read the final piece of advice below that Magdalena gives to Rosario. Answer the questions in English that follow.

> *Si la situación no es mejor después de unas semanas, tienes que considerar la posibilidad de separar el dormitorio con una cortina. ¡Pero no debe ser una cortina ni negra ni amarilla!*

1. How long does Magdalena tell Rosario to wait before considering another possibility?

   _____

2. According to Magdalena, with what should Rosario separate the room?

   _____

3. What colors should not separate the two rooms?

   _____ and _____

**D.** In your own words, explain what the disaster in Rosario's bedroom is.

_____

_____

**Realidades B**

**Capítulo 6A**

Nombre _____

Fecha _____

Hora _____

**Guided Practice Activities 6A-6**

# Presentación oral (p. 119)

**Task:** Use a photograph or drawing of a bedroom to talk about what its contents and colors tell about the personality of the owner.

**A.** Bring in a picture of a bedroom. It can be a photo, a picture cut out from a magazine, or a picture that you drew. Use the following four questions to organize your thoughts about the room. Write your answers to the questions on the line beneath each question.

1. ¿Qué hay en el dormitorio?

   _____

2. ¿Cómo es el dormitorio?

   _____

3. ¿De qué color es?

   _____

4. ¿Qué cosas hay en las paredes?

   _____

**B.** Using the information you just compiled in **part A**, answer the questions below in the spaces provided.

- En tu opinión, ¿cómo es la persona que vive (*lives*) en el dormitorio?
- ¿Qué le gusta hacer?

Es una persona _____ porque el dormitorio _____

_____ .

Le gusta _____ porque en el dormitorio hay _____

_____ .

**C.** Go through your presentation several times. Make sure you:

_____ support your statements with examples

_____ use complete sentences

_____ speak clearly

**Realidades** Ⓑ

**Capítulo 6B**

Nombre _____

Fecha _____

Hora _____

**Vocabulary Flash Cards, Sheet 1**

Write the Spanish vocabulary word below each picture. If there is a word or phrase, copy it in the space provided. Be sure to include the article for each noun.

| | | |
|---|---|---|
| _____ _____ | _____ _____ | _____ _____ |
| _____ _____ | _____ _____ | _____ _____ |
| _____ _____ | _____ _____ | _____ _____ |

**Realidades** **B**

**Capítulo 6B**

Nombre _____

Fecha _____

Hora _____

**Vocabulary Flash Cards, Sheet 2**

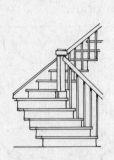

_____

_____

_____

_____

_____

_____

_____

_____

_____

_____

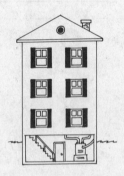

_____

_____

**el
piso**

_____

_____

_____

_____

_____

_____

**Realidades** **B**

**Capítulo 6B**

Nombre _____

Fecha _____

Hora _____

**Vocabulary Flash Cards, Sheet 3**

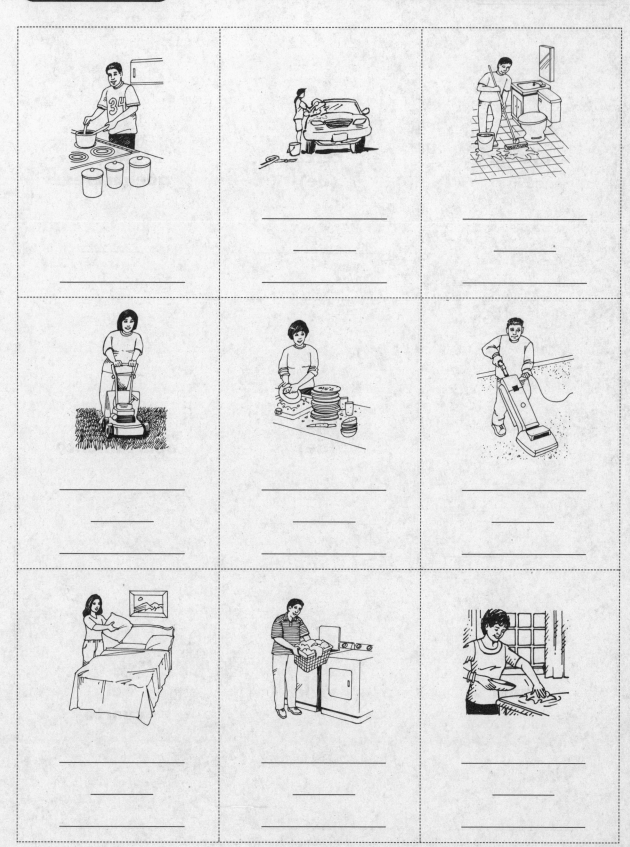

| | | |
|---|---|---|
| ayudar<br><br>_____ | cerca<br>(de)<br><br>_____ | los<br>quehaceres<br><br>_____ |
| dar<br><br>_____ | lejos<br>(de)<br><br>_____ | el<br>apartamento<br><br>_____ |
| poner<br><br>_____ | vivir<br><br>_____ | el<br>cuarto<br><br>_____ |

**Realidades** B

**Capítulo 6B**

Nombre _____

Fecha _____

Hora _____

**Vocabulary Flash Cards, Sheet 5**

| | | |
|---|---|---|
| sucio, sucia<br><br>_____ ,<br>_____ | ¿Qué estás haciendo?<br><br>_____<br>_____<br>_____ | si<br><br><br><br>_____ |
| bastante<br><br><br><br>_____ | un momento<br><br><br>_____<br><br>_____ | <br><br><br><br>_____ |
| ¿Cuáles?<br><br><br><br>_____ | recibir<br><br><br><br>_____ | <br><br><br>_____<br><br>_____ |

_____
_____

_____
_____

_____
_____

_____
_____

_____
_____

_____
_____

_____
_____

_____
_____

_____
_____

Tear out this page. Write the English words on the lines. Fold the paper along the dotted line to see the correct answers so you can check your work.

cerca (de)  _____

lejos (de)  _____

vivir  _____

el apartamento  _____

la cocina  _____

el comedor  _____

el despacho  _____

la escalera  _____

el garaje  _____

la planta baja  _____

el primer piso  _____

el segundo piso  _____

la sala  _____

el sótano  _____

arreglar el cuarto  _____

_____

ayudar  _____

cocinar  _____

cortar el césped  _____

Fold In →

**Realidades B**

**Capítulo 6B**

Nombre _____

Fecha _____

Hora _____

**Vocabulary Check, Sheet 2**

Tear out this page. Write the Spanish words on the lines. Fold the paper along the dotted line to see the correct answers so you can check your work.

close (to), near _____

far (from) _____

to live _____

apartment _____

kitchen _____

dining room _____

home office _____

stairs, stairway _____

garage _____

ground floor _____

second floor _____

third floor _____

living room _____

basement _____

to straighten up
the room _____

to help _____

to cook _____

to cut the lawn _____

Fold In

Tear out this page. Write the English words on the lines. Fold the paper along the dotted line to see the correct answers so you can check your work.

dar de comer
al perro                    _____

hacer la cama              _____

lavar los platos           _____

limpiar el baño            _____

                           _____

pasar la
aspiradora                 _____

poner la mesa              _____

los quehaceres             _____

quitar el polvo            _____

sacar la basura            _____

                           _____

limpio, limpia             _____

sucio, sucia               _____

bastante                   _____

el dinero                  _____

recibir                    _____

Fold In

**Realidades** **B**

**Capítulo 6B**

Nombre _____

Hora _____

Fecha _____

**Vocabulary Check, Sheet 4**

Tear out this page. Write the Spanish words on the lines. Fold the paper along the dotted line to see the correct answers so you can check your work.

to feed the dog          _____

_____

to make the bed          _____

to wash the dishes          _____

to clean the bathroom          _____

to vacuum          _____

_____

to set the table          _____

chores          _____

to dust          _____

to take out the trash          _____

clean          _____

dirty          _____

enough; rather          _____

money          _____

to receive          _____

Fold In

To hear a complete list of the vocabulary for this chapter, go to Disc 2, Track 4 on the Guided Practice Audio CD, or go to www.phschool.com and type in the Web Code jcd-0699. Then click on **Repaso del capítulo.**

# Affirmative *tú* commands (p. 138)

- **Tú** commands are used to tell friends, family members, or peers to do something.
- **Tú** command forms are the same as the regular present-tense forms for **Ud./él/ella.**

| Infinitive | *Ud./él/ella* form | Affirmative *tú* command |
|---|---|---|
| **-ar** verb: **hablar** | habla | **¡Habla!** |
| **-er** verb: **leer** | lee | **¡Lee!** |
| **-ir** verb: **escribir** | escribe | **¡Escribe!** |

- Two verbs you have learned already, **hacer** and **poder**, have irregular affirmative **tú** command forms:

  poner → **pon**     **¡Pon** la mesa!
  hacer → **haz**     **¡Haz** la cama!

- You can tell the difference between a command form and an **Ud., él,** or **ella** verb form from the context of the sentence. A comma after the person's name indicates they are being talked to directly. Possessive adjectives can also help you decide if the person is being addressed directly (**tu**) or referred to in the third person (**su**).

  Marcos lee **su** libro. (**él** verb form)
  Marcos, lee **tu** libro. (command form)

**A.** Circle the command form in each sentence.

1. María, habla con tu hermano, por favor.
2. Tomasina, escribe tu tarea.
3. Marcos, come el almuerzo.
4. Silvia, practica la guitarra.

5. Elena, haz la cama.
6. Sandra, pon la mesa.
7. Alfonso, lee el libro.
8. Carlos, lava el coche.

**B.** Now look at each sentence. Write **C** if the verb is a command form. Write **no** if it is not a command form. Follow the models.

Modelos   Javier estudia en su dormitorio.      *no*
          Javier, estudia en tu dormitorio.     *C*

1. Alfonso lee el libro. _____
2. Paula, ayuda a tu madre. _____
3. Roberto escucha a su madre. _____
4. Pablo hace la tarea. _____

5. Ana, lava los platos. _____
6. Isa juega con su hermana. _____
7. David, limpia la casa. _____
8. Elena, pon la mesa. _____

**Realidades** B

**Capítulo 6B**

Nombre _____

Hora _____

Fecha _____

**Guided Practice Activities 6B-2**

# Affirmative *tú* commands (*continued*)

**C.** Circle the correct form of the verb to complete each sentence.

1. ¡(**Plancha** / **Planchan**) la ropa, por favor!

2. Gerardo, (**prepara** / **preparas**) la comida, por favor.

3. Alberto, (**hace** / **haz**) la tarea ahora.

4. Rosa, (**pone** / **pon**) los platos en la mesa, por favor.

5. ¡(**Lavas** / **Lava**) el coche, por favor!

6. Linda, (**juega** / **juegas**) con tu hermana esta tarde.

**D.** Write the affirmative **tú** command forms to complete the following conversations. Follow the model.

**Modelo**  RAÚL:  Ana, (**poner**) ____*pon*____ los libros en la mesa.

  ANA:  Sí, pero (**tomar**) ___*toma*___ mi mochila.

1. SEBASTIÁN:  Roberto, (**lavar**) _____ los platos, por favor.

  ROBERTO:  Claro. (**Traer**) _____ los platos sucios aquí.

2. TERESA:  Susana, (**preparar**) _____ el almuerzo.

  SUSANA:  Sí, pero (**hablar**) _____ con mamá para ver qué necesitamos.

3. EDUARDO:  Elena, (**hacer**) _____ los quehaceres.

  ELENA:  Claro. (**Escribir**) _____ una lista.

4. ISABEL:  Margarita, (**planchar**) _____ la ropa, por favor.

  MARGARITA:  Claro, pero (**sacar**) _____ la plancha, por favor.

**E.** Write **tú** command forms to complete each sentence. Use verbs from the list.

| hacer | lavar | poner | sacar |
|-------|-------|-------|-------|

1. ¡_____ la basura!

2. ¡_____ el coche!

3. ¡_____ la mesa!

4. ¡_____ la cama!

Go Online WEB CODE jcd-0613
PHSchool.com

**Realidades**  **B**

**Capítulo 6B**

Nombre _____

Fecha _____

Hora _____

**Guided Practice Activities 6B-3**

## The present progressive tense (p. 142)

- Use the present progressive tense to say what people are doing or what is happening right now.

   **Estamos lavando** el coche.    *We are washing the car.*

- The present progressive tense uses forms of **estar** with the present participle.

- Review the forms of **estar**:

| yo | estoy | nosotros/nosotras | estamos |
|---|---|---|---|
| tú | estás | vosotros/vosotras | estáis |
| usted/él/ella | está | ustedes/ellos/ellas | están |

- You form the present participle for **-ar** verbs by removing the **-ar** ending and adding **-ando**: **preparar → preparando, hablar → hablando.**

- You form the present participle for **-er** and **-ir** verbs by removing the **-er** or **-ir** ending and adding **-iendo: comer → comiendo, escribir → escribiendo.**

- The forms of **estar** change to match the subject of the sentence. The present participle always stays the same, regardless of who the subject is.

   Francisco <u>está</u> <u>limpiando</u> la mesa.    *Francisco is cleaning the table.*

   **Tú y yo** <u>estamos</u> <u>limpiando</u> el baño.    *We are cleaning the bathroom.*

**A.** Look at each sentence. Underline the form of **estar.** Circle the present participle. Follow the model.

**Modelo**   Enrique <u>está</u> (lavando) los platos.

1. Tú y yo estamos pasando la aspiradora.

2. Mis abuelos están cortando el césped.

3. Mi hermana está quitando el polvo en la sala.

4. Yo estoy dando de comer al perro.

5. Ustedes están sacando la basura de la cocina.

6. Tú estás poniendo la mesa con los platos limpios.

7. Ella está haciendo las camas del segundo piso.

**B.** Complete each sentence with the appropriate form of **estar.**

1. Yo _____ poniendo la mesa.

2. Tú _____ sacando la basura.

3. Ella _____ lavando la ropa.

4. Nosotros _____ preparando el almuerzo.

5. Ustedes _____ cortando el césped.

# The present progressive tense *(continued)*

**C.** Write the present participles of the verbs shown. Follow the models. Remember to use **-ando** for **-ar** verbs and **-iendo** for **-er** and **-ir** verbs.

| Modelos | ayudar | *ayudando* |
| | hacer | *haciendo* |
| | escribir | *escribiendo* |

1. dar _____
2. abrir _____
3. comer _____
4. romper _____

5. sacar _____
6. lavar _____
7. jugar _____
8. poner _____

**D.** Look at the drawing. Then write forms of the present progressive (**estar** + present participle) to complete each sentence. Follow the models.

Modelos   Graciela (**dar**) _____*está dando*_____ de comer al perro.

Lola y Elia (**hablar**) _____*están hablando*_____ .

1. El padre (**sacar**) _____ la basura.
2. La madre (**cocinar**) _____ unas hamburguesas.
3. Ana María (**cortar**) _____ el césped.
4. Manolo y José (**lavar**) _____ el coche.
5. Tito y Ramón (**poner**) _____ la mesa.

Go Online WEB CODE jcd-0614
PHSchool.com

**Realidades B**

**Capítulo 6B**

Nombre _____

Fecha _____

Hora _____

**Guided Practice Activities 6B-5**

## Lectura: Cantaclara (pp. 146–147)

**A.** The reading in your textbook is similar to the story of Cinderella. Write four facts that you can remember about the Cinderella story in the spaces below. If you are not familiar with the story you will need to find out from someone who is.

1. _____
2. _____
3. _____
4. _____

**B.** Skim through the reading and the pictures in your textbook to find similarities between the story of Cantaclara and Cinderella. Check off any similarities in your list above.

**C.** Since you know that the story in your textbook is like the story of Cinderella, you know that Cantaclara lives with her stepmother and two stepsisters. Below is a dialogue with all four of them. Read the dialogue and answer the questions that follow.

> –Cantaclara, saca la basura. Y después, pon la mesa –dice la madrastra.
> –Cantaclara, haz mi cama y limpia el baño –dice Griselda.
> –Haz mi cama también –dice Hortencia.
> –Un momento. Estoy lavando los platos ahora mismo –dice Cantaclara.

1. Circle the names of the four people who are speaking.
2. How is a dialogue written differently in Spanish than in English?

_____

3. Which person does NOT say she wants Cantaclara to make her bed?

_____

**D.** Now, read what takes place at the end of the story. Answer the questions in English that follow.

> Son las ocho de la noche. La madrastra y las dos hermanastras están en la sala y ven su programa favorito. Pero, ¿qué es esto? ¡Ven a Cantaclara en la pantalla!
> –Mira, mamá. ¡Es Cantaclara! –dice Hortencia.
> –¡Oh, no! Si Cantaclara es la nueva estrella del futuro, ¿quién va a hacer los quehaceres? –pregunta Griselda.

1. At what time do the stepmother and stepsisters sit down to watch their favorite show? _____
2. Whom do they see on TV? _____
3. What problem does Griselda think of at the end? _____

**Realidades B**

**Capítulo 6B**

Nombre _____

Hora _____

Fecha _____

**Guided Practice Activities 6B-6**

# Presentación escrita (p. 149)

**Task:** Pretend that your family is selling their house, apartment, or that you are selling an imaginary dream home. Create a flyer in Spanish to promote the sale of your home.

**❶ Prewrite.** You are going to prepare an informative flyer about your home. In order to provide the most information to potential buyers, you will need to anticipate their questions. Read the potential questions below and write answers about your home in the spaces provided.

a) En general, ¿cómo es la casa o apartamento? (¿Es grande o pequeño?)

_____.

b) ¿De qué color es la casa o apartamento?

_____.

c) ¿Cuántos cuartos hay en la casa o apartamento? ¿Cuáles son?

_____.

d) ¿Cómo son los cuartos? (¿grandes o pequeños?)

_____.

e) ¿De qué color son los cuartos?

_____.

f) ¿Cuál es la dirección (*address*) y el precio (*price*) de la casa o apartamento?

_____.

**❷ Draft.** Now, compile the answers you wrote above on a separate sheet of paper to create your rough draft. Organize your answers in a way that will be easy for anyone to read. Your flyer should also include illustrations and colored ink to make it more attractive to potential buyers. The first line on your flyer should read: **Se vende casa** (or **Se vende apartamento**).

**❸ Revise.** Read through your ad to see that you have included all the information that a potential buyer might want. Share your draft with a partner who will check the following:

_____ Are all words spelled correctly?

_____ Is the flyer neat and attractive?

_____ Does the flyer need a visual?

_____ Is the key information provided?

_____ Does the flyer make me want to look at the property?

**❹ Publish.** Write a new, final copy of your flyer making any necessary corrections or adding to it anything your partner suggested.

# Cap Realidades B

Nombre _____ Hora _____

Fecha _____ **Vocabulary Flash Cards, Sheet 1**

Write the Spanish vocabulary word below each picture. If there is a word or phrase, copy it in the space provided. Be sure to include the article for each noun.

_____   _____   _____

_____   _____   _____

_____   _____   _____

*Guided Practice Activities* — *Vocabulary Flash Cards 7A* **213**

© Pearson Education, Inc. All rights reserved.

**Realidades**

**Capítulo 7A**

Nombre _____

Hora _____

Fecha _____

**Vocabulary Flash Cards, Sheet 2**

_____

_____

_____

_____

_____

_____

_____

_____

_____

_____

_____

_____

_____

**Realidades** Ⓑ

**Capítulo 7A**

Nombre _____

Hora _____

Fecha _____

**Vocabulary Flash Cards, Sheet 3**

buscar

_____

la
tienda

_____

_____

comprar

_____

la tienda
de ropa

_____

_____

entrar

_____

¿En qué
puedo
servirle?

_____ _____

_____

llevar

| nuevo, nueva | Me queda(n) mal. | ¡Vamos! |
|---|---|---|
| _____ , _____ | _____ _____ _____ | _____ |
| ¿Cómo te queda(n)? | quizás | costar |
| _____ _____ | _____ | _____ |
| Me queda(n) bien. | Perdón. | ¿Cuánto cuesta(n)...? |
| _____ _____ | _____ | _____ _____ |

| el precio | trescientos, trescientas | seiscientos, seiscientas |
|---|---|---|
| ___ | ___ | ___ |
| tanto | cuatrocientos, cuatrocientas | setecientos, setecientas |
| ___ | ___ | ___ |
| doscientos, doscientas | quinientos, quinientas | ochocientos, ochocientas |
| ___ | ___ | ___ |

| novecientos, novecientas | los dos | estos, estas |
|---|---|---|
| _____ _____ | _____ | _____ _____ |
| mil | las dos | ese, esa |
| _____ | _____ | _____ |
| tener razón | este, esta | esos, esas |
| _____ | _____ | _____ |

**Realidades B**

**Capítulo 7A**

Nombre _____

Fecha _____

Hora _____

**Vocabulary Check, Sheet 1**

Tear out this page. Write the English words on the lines. Fold the paper along the dotted line to see the correct answers so you can check your work.

buscar            _____

comprar         _____

el dependiente,     _____
la dependienta

entrar             _____

la tienda de ropa    _____

el abrigo          _____

la blusa           _____

las botas          _____

los calcetines      _____

la camiseta        _____

la chaqueta        _____

la falda           _____

la gorra           _____

los jeans          _____

los pantalones     _____
cortos

la sudadera        _____

el suéter          _____

Fold In

Nombre _____ Hora _____

Fecha _____ **Vocabulary Check, Sheet 2**

Tear out this page. Write the Spanish words on the lines. Fold the paper along the dotted line to see the correct answers so you can check your work.

to look for _____

to buy _____

salesperson _____

_____

to enter _____

clothing store _____

coat _____

blouse _____

boots _____

socks _____

T-shirt _____

jacket _____

skirt _____

cap _____

jeans _____

shorts _____

_____

sweatshirt _____

sweater _____

Fold In

**Realidades** Ⓑ

Nombre _____

Hora _____

**Capítulo 7A**

Fecha _____

**Vocabulary Check, Sheet 3**

Tear out this page. Write the English words on the lines. Fold the paper along the dotted line to see the correct answers so you can check your work.

el traje de baño _____

el vestido _____

los zapatos _____

llevar _____

nuevo, nueva _____

costar _____

el precio _____

doscientos _____

trescientos _____

cuatrocientos _____

quinientos _____

seiscientos _____

setecientos _____

ochocientos _____

novecientos _____

mil _____

tener razón _____

Fold In

Nombre _____

Hora _____

Fecha _____

**Vocabulary Check, Sheet 4**

Tear out this page. Write the Spanish words on the lines. Fold the paper along the dotted line to see the correct answers so you can check your work.

swimsuit _____

dress _____

shoes _____

to wear _____

new _____

to cost _____

price _____

two hundred _____

three hundred _____

four hundred _____

five hundred _____

six hundred _____

seven hundred _____

eight hundred _____

nine hundred _____

a thousand _____

to be correct _____

Fold In

To hear a complete list of the vocabulary for this chapter, go to Disc 2, Track 5 on the Guided Practice Audio CD, or go to www.phschool.com and type in the Web Code jcd-0789. Then click on **Repaso del capítulo.**

**Realidades B**

**Capítulo 7A**

Nombre _____

Fecha _____

Hora _____

**Guided Practice Activities 7A-1**

# Stem-changing verbs: *pensar, querer, preferir* (p. 168)

- Like the other stem-changing verbs you've learned (**jugar**, **poder**, and **dormir**), **pensar**, **querer**, and **preferir** use the regular present-tense endings. These endings attach to a new stem for all forms except for the **nosotros** and **vosotros** forms, which use the existing stem.

- Here are the forms of **pensar**, **querer**, and **preferir**. Note that in all cases, the **e** in the stem changes to **ie**.

| yo | **pienso** | nosotros/nosotras | **pensamos** |
|---|---|---|---|
| tú | **piensas** | vosotros/vosotras | **pensáis** |
| usted/él/ella | **piensa** | ustedes/ellos/ellas | **piensan** |

| yo | **quiero** | nosotros/nosotras | **queremos** |
|---|---|---|---|
| tú | **quieres** | vosotros/vosotras | **queréis** |
| usted/él/ella | **quiere** | ustedes/ellos/ellas | **quieren** |

| yo | **prefiero** | nosotros/nosotras | **preferimos** |
|---|---|---|---|
| tú | **prefieres** | vosotros/vosotras | **preferís** |
| usted/él/ella | **prefiere** | ustedes/ellos/ellas | **prefieren** |

**A.** Circle the forms of **pensar**, **querer**, or **preferir** in each sentence. Then underline the stem in each verb you circled. The first one has been done for you.

1. (Prefieren) comprar unos zapatos.

2. Queremos ir de compras.

3. Pensamos ir a la tienda de ropa.

4. ¿Prefiere Ud. el vestido o la falda?

5. Pienso comprar una sudadera.

6. ¿Quieres hablar con la dependienta?

7. Preferimos ir a una tienda grande.

8. Quieren entrar en la tienda.

**B.** Now, write the forms of **pensar**, **querer**, and **preferir** that you circled in **part A** next to each subject pronoun.

1. ellos (preferir) _____

2. nosotros (querer) _____

3. nosotros (pensar) _____

4. Ud. (preferir) _____

5. yo (pensar) _____

6. tú (querer) _____

7. nosotros (preferir) _____

8. ellos (querer) _____

**Realidades B**

**Capítulo 7A**

Nombre _____

Fecha _____

Hora _____

**Guided Practice Activities 7A-2**

# Stem-changing verbs (continued)

**C.** Circle the correct form of **pensar, querer,** or **preferir** to complete each sentence.

1. Yo ( **quiere** / **quiero** ) comprar unas botas nuevas.

2. Ella ( **prefiere** / **prefieren** ) los pantalones cortos a la falda.

3. Nosotros ( **prefieren** / **preferimos** ) ir de compras en una tienda grande.

4. Ellos ( **pienso** / **piensan** ) comprar dos abrigos nuevos.

5. Tú y yo ( **pensamos** / **piensas** ) buscar una tienda con precios buenos.

6. Ustedes ( **quieres** / **quieren** ) hablar con la dependienta.

7. Nosotros ( **queremos** / **quieres** ) entrar en la tienda de ropa.

8. Tú y yo no ( **piensan** / **pensamos** ) comprar ropa hoy.

**D.** Complete the sentences with forms of **pensar, querer,** or **preferir.** Follow the models.

Modelos   Tú (**pensar**) comprar un suéter.

Tú _____*piensas*_____ comprar un suéter.

Tú y yo (**preferir**) comprar el vestido azul.

Tú y yo ___*preferimos*___ comprar el vestido azul.

1. Elena (**pensar**) comprar una sudadera.

Elena _____ comprar una sudadera.

2. Sandra y yo (**querer**) ir a una tienda de ropa grande.

Sandra y yo _____ ir a una tienda de ropa grande.

3. Yo (**preferir**) hablar con un dependiente.

Yo _____ hablar con un dependiente.

4. Nosotras (**pensar**) que es un precio bueno.

Nosotras _____ que es un precio bueno.

5. Tú (**querer**) entrar en una tienda de ropa grande.

Tú _____ entrar en una tienda de ropa grande.

6. Tú y yo (**querer**) comprar unas camisetas nuevas.

Tú y yo _____ comprar unas camisetas nuevas.

7. Tomás y Sebastián (**preferir**) no comprar ropa hoy.

Tomás y Sebastián _____ no comprar ropa hoy.

8. Yo (**pensar**) comprar una gorra y un suéter.

Yo _____ comprar una gorra y un suéter.

**Go Online** WEB CODE jcd-0704
**PHSchool.com**

**Realidades** Ⓑ

**Capítulo 7A**

Nombre _____

Fecha _____

Hora _____

**Guided Practice Activities 7A-3**

# Demonstrative adjectives (p. 172)

- Demonstrative adjectives are the equivalent of **this, that, these,** and **those** in English. You use them to point out nouns: **this hat, those shoes**.
- In Spanish, the demonstrative adjectives agree with the noun they accompany in both gender and number.

| | Close | | Farther away | |
|---|---|---|---|---|
| **Singular masculine** | **este** suéter | (**this** sweater) | **ese** suéter | (**that** sweater) |
| **Singular feminine** | **esta** falda | (**this** skirt) | **esa** falda | (**that** skirt) |
| **Plural masculine** | **estos** suéteres | (**these** sweaters) | **esos** suéteres | (**those** sweaters) |
| **Plural feminine** | **estas** faldas | (**these** skirts) | **esas** faldas | (**those** skirts) |

**A.** Circle the demonstrative adjective in each sentence below. Write **C** next to the sentence if the object referred to is *close* (**este, esta, estos, estas**). Write **F** if the object referred to is *farther away* (**ese, esa, esos, esas**).

1. Me gustan estos zapatos. _____

2. Quiero comprar esas camisetas. _____

3. ¿Prefieres esta falda? _____

4. Esa camisa es muy bonita. _____

5. No me gustan esos vestidos. _____

6. ¿Te gustan estas chaquetas? _____

**B.** Circle the correct demonstrative adjective in each sentence.

1. ¿Cómo me quedan ( **esto** / **estos** ) pantalones?

2. Me gustan ( **esas** / **esos** ) sudaderas.

3. ¿Prefieres ( **esta** / **este** ) chaqueta?

4. Pienso comprar ( **estos** / **este** ) calcetines.

5. No me gusta ( **ese** / **esa** ) abrigo.

6. ¿Cómo me queda ( **este** / **esta** ) traje?

7. ( **Eso** / **Esas** ) botas son muy bonitas.

8. ¿Vas a comprar ( **esos** / **esas** ) pantalones cortos?

# Demonstrative adjectives (*continued*)

**C.** Choose the correct form of the demonstrative adjective and write it next to each noun. Follow the models.

**Close: este, esta, estos, estas    Farther: ese, esa, esos, esas**

Modelos  calcetines (close): _____*estos*_____ calcetines

camisa (farther): _____*esa*_____ camisa

1. abrigo (farther): _____ abrigo

2. botas (farther): _____ botas

3. jeans (close): _____ jeans

4. falda (close): _____ falda

5. traje de baño (close): _____ traje de baño

6. zapatos (farther): _____ zapatos

7. chaquetas (farther): _____ chaquetas

8. pantalones (close): _____ pantalones

9. vestido (farther): _____ vestido

10. suéter (close): _____ suéter

**D.** In each drawing below, the item of clothing that is larger is closer to you. The one that is smaller is farther away. Write the correct demonstrative adjective to indicate the item that is marked with an arrow. Follow the model.

Modelo  _____*esta*_____ camisa

1.  _____ pantalones    4.  _____ zapatos

2.  _____ sudaderas    5.  _____ abrigo

3.  _____ vestido

**Go Online** WEB CODE jcd-0703
**PHSchool.com**

**Realidades** B

Nombre _____

Hora _____

**Capítulo 7A**

Fecha _____

**Guided Practice Activities 7A-5**

## Lectura: Tradiciones de la ropa panameña (pp. 176–177)

**A.** You will find out a lot about the contents of the reading in your textbook by looking at the title and the photos. In the spaces below, write three main topics that you would expect a reading on Panamanian culture to cover.

1. _____

2. _____

3. _____

**B.** Read the paragraph below on **polleras** and answer the questions that follow in Spanish.

> *Una tradición panameña de mucho orgullo (pride) es llevar el vestido típico de las mujeres, "la pollera". Hay dos tipos de pollera, la pollera montuna y la pollera de gala, que se lleva en los festivales.*

1. Según la lectura, ¿cómo se llama el vestido típico de las mujeres en Panamá?

_____

2. ¿Cuáles son los dos tipos de pollera?

_____ y _____

3. ¿Cuándo se lleva la pollera de gala? _____

**C.** Look through the reading in your textbook again to find whether the following statements are true or false. Then, circle **cierto** for true or **falso** for false.

1. **cierto** **falso** Hay un Día Nacional de la Pollera en la ciudad de Las Tablas.

2. **cierto** **falso** Las Tablas es famosa por ser el mejor lugar para celebrar los carnavales.

3. **cierto** **falso** El canal de Panamá conecta el océano Pacífico con el lago Titicaca.

4. **cierto** **falso** Panamá es un istmo.

5. **cierto** **falso** El segundo tipo de ropa auténtico de Panamá que se menciona es la gorra de Panamá.

# Presentación oral (p. 179)

**Task:** You and a partner will play the roles of a customer and a salesclerk. The customer will look at various items in the store, talk with the clerk, and then decide if he or she would like to buy anything.

**A.** Work with a partner to prepare the skit. You will be the customer. You and your partner will need to discuss what type of clothing your store is selling. You will then need a name for your store and some samples of merchandise to use in your skit. You may bring in clothes or use cutouts from a magazine. Complete the following in the spaces below:

Type of clothing: _____

Store name: _____

**B.** Now, make a list below of five different expressions and questions that will help you play your role. You may want to look back in the *A primera vista* and *Videohistoria* sections in your textbook for ideas to help you get started.

1. _____
2. _____
3. _____
4. _____
5. _____

**C.** Work with your partner to put together and practice your presentation. Keep in mind the following things:

_____ to answer questions using complete sentences

_____ to speak clearly

_____ to keep the conversation going

_____ to finish the conversation at a logical point

**D.** When you present your skit, the clerk will begin the conversation. That means that you will need to respond as your first action. As your last action, you will need to decide whether or not to buy something. Your teacher will grade you based on the following:

• how well you keep the conversation going

• how complete your presentation is

• how well you use new and previously learned vocabulary

**Realidades B**

**Capítulo 7B**

Nombre _____

Fecha _____

Hora _____

**Vocabulary Flash Cards, Sheet 1**

Write the Spanish vocabulary word below each picture. If there is a word or phrase, copy it in the space provided. Be sure to include the article for each noun.

**Realidades**  **B**

**Capítulo 7B**

Nombre _____

Hora _____

Fecha _____

**Vocabulary Flash Cards, Sheet 2**

_____

_____

_____

_____

**en la
Red**

_____  _____

_____

_____

_____

_____

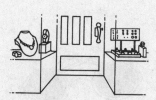

_____

_____

_____

_____

_____

_____

"Almacén Galerías"

_____

_____

_____

_____

**Realidades B**

**Capítulo 7B**

Nombre

Fecha

Hora

**Vocabulary Flash Cards, Sheet 3**

el
novio

caro,
cara

_____ ,

la
novia

_____

mirar

barato,
barata

_____ ,

pagar
(por)

**Realidades** Ⓑ

**Capítulo 7B**

Nombre _____

Fecha _____

Hora _____

**Vocabulary Flash Cards, Sheet 4**

vender

_____

ayer

_____

hace
+ *time*
*expression*

_____

_____

anoche

_____

la semana
pasada

_____  _____

_____

_____

_____

el año
pasado

_____

_____

¡Uf!

_____

_____

_____

_____

**Realidades B**

**Capítulo 7B**

Nombre _____

Fecha _____

Hora _____

**Vocabulary Check, Sheet 1**

Tear out this page. Write the English words on the lines. Fold the paper along the dotted line to see the correct answers so you can check your work.

el almacén

_____

en la Red                    _____

la joyería                   _____

la librería                  _____

la tienda de                 _____
descuentos

la tienda de                 _____
electrodomésticos            _____

la zapatería                 _____

el anillo                    _____

los anteojos de sol          _____

los aretes                   _____

el bolso                     _____

la cadena                    _____

la cartera                   _____

el collar                    _____

la corbata                   _____

los guantes                  _____

el llavero                   _____

Fold In

Tear out this page. Write the Spanish words on the lines. Fold the paper along the dotted line to see the correct answers so you can check your work.

| | |
|---|---|
| department store | _el almacén_ |
| online | _en la Red_ |
| jewelry store | _la joyería_ |
| bookstore | _la librería_ |
| discount store | _la tienda de descuentos_ |
| household appliance store | _la tienda de electrodomésticos_ |
| shoe store | _la zapatería_ |
| ring | _el anillo_ |
| sunglasses | _los anteojos de sol_ |
| earrings | _los aretes_ |
| purse | _el bolso_ |
| chain | _la cadena_ |
| wallet | _la cartera_ |
| necklace | _el collar_ |
| tie | _la corbata_ |
| gloves | _los guantes_ |
| key chain | _el llavero_ |

Fold In →

Nombre _____ Hora _____

Fecha _____ **Vocabulary Check, Sheet 3**

Tear out this page. Write the English words on the lines. Fold the paper along the dotted line to see the correct answers so you can check your work.

el perfume _____

la pulsera _____

el reloj pulsera _____

el software _____

el novio _____

la novia _____

barato, _____
barata _____

caro, cara _____

mirar _____

pagar (por) _____

vender _____

Fold In

Nombre _____

Hora _____

Fecha _____

Tear out this page. Write the Spanish words on the lines. Fold the paper along the dotted line to see the correct answers so you can check your work.

perfume _____

bracelet _____

watch _____

software _____

boyfriend _____

girlfriend _____

inexpensive, cheap _____

expensive _____

to look (at) _____

to pay (for) _____

to sell _____

Fold In ←

To hear a complete list of the vocabulary for this chapter, go to Disc 2, Track 6 on the Guided Practice Audio CD, or go to www.phschool.com and type in the Web Code jcd-0799. Then click on **Repaso del capítulo.**

**Realidades** (B)

**Capítulo 7B**

Nombre _____

Hora _____

Fecha _____

**Guided Practice Activities 7B-1**

# The preterite of -ar verbs (p. 196)

- The preterite is a Spanish past tense that is used to talk about actions that were completed in the past: *I went to the store. I bought a jacket.*
- To form the preterite of **-ar** verbs, you take the stem of the verb (the same stem you used to form the present tense) and add the following endings:

**hablar → habl-** + endings

| yo | **hablé** | nosotros/nosotras | **hablamos** |
|---|---|---|---|
| tú | **hablaste** | vosotros/vosotras | **hablasteis** |
| usted/él/ella | **habló** | ustedes/ellos/ellas | **hablaron** |

- Notice the accents on the **yo** and **usted/él/ella** forms: **hablé**, **habló**.

**A.** Underline the preterite verb forms in the following conversations. **¡Ojo!** Not all the verb forms are preterite forms.

1. ELENA:   ¿Hablaste con Enrique ayer?

   ANA:   Sí, hablamos por teléfono anoche. Él trabajó ayer.

   ELENA:   ¿Ah, sí? ¿Dónde trabaja?

   ANA:   Trabaja en un restaurante. Ayer lavó muchos platos y limpió las mesas.

2. MARCOS:   ¿Estudiaste para el examen?

   TOMÁS:   Sí, estudié mucho, pero estoy nervioso.

   MARCOS:   Yo también. Pasé dos horas en la biblioteca.

   TOMÁS:   Yo estudié en casa y usé la computadora.

**B.** Now, fill in the conversations from **part B** with the missing preterite forms.

1. ELENA:   ¿_____ con Enrique ayer?

   ANA:   Sí, _____ por teléfono anoche. Él _____ ayer.

   ELENA:   ¿Ah, sí? ¿Dónde trabaja?

   ANA:   Trabaja en un restaurante. Ayer _____ muchos platos

   y _____ las mesas.

2. MARCOS:   ¿_____ para el examen?

   TOMÁS:   Sí, _____ mucho, pero estoy nervioso.

   MARCOS:   Yo también. _____ dos horas en la biblioteca.

   TOMÁS:   Yo _____ en casa y _____ la computadora.

**Realidades B**

**Capítulo 7B**

Nombre _____

Fecha _____

Hora _____

**Guided Practice Activities 7B-2**

# The preterite of -ar verbs (continued)

**C.** Circle the correct preterite form to complete each sentence.

1. Yo ( **caminó** / **caminé** ) por dos horas ayer.

2. Ellos ( **hablaste** / **hablaron** ) por teléfono anoche.

3. Nosotros ( **cocinamos** / **cocinaron** ) la cena.

4. Tú ( **cantaron** / **cantaste** ) en la ópera.

5. Ella ( **escuchó** / **escucharon** ) música en su dormitorio.

6. Ustedes ( **levantaron** / **levantamos** ) pesas en el gimnasio.

**D.** Write the missing preterite forms in the chart.

|  | cantar | bailar | escuchar | lavar | nadar |
|---|---|---|---|---|---|
| yo | canté |  |  |  |  |
| tú |  | bailaste |  |  |  |
| Ud./él/ella |  |  | escuchó |  |  |
| nosotros/nosotras |  |  |  | lavamos |  |
| Uds./ellos/ellas |  |  |  |  | nadaron |

**E.** Write the correct preterite form of the verb indicated next to each subject pronoun. Follow the model.

**Modelo** tú (bailar) _____*bailaste*_____

1. yo (cantar) _____
2. ella (nadar) _____
3. Ud. (esquiar) _____
4. ellos (lavar) _____
5. nosotros (dibujar) _____
6. ellos (pasar) _____
7. tú (hablar) _____
8. yo (limpiar) _____

**F.** Use verbs from the list to say what you and your friends did last night.

> estudiar   trabajar   hablar por teléfono   bailar   cantar   cocinar
> escuchar música   esquiar   lavar la ropa   levantar pesas   limpiar el baño

1. Anoche yo _____.

2. Yo no _____.

3. Anoche mis amigos _____.

4. Nosotros no _____.

**Go Online** WEB CODE jcd-0713
**PHSchool.com**

**Realidades B**

**Capítulo 7B**

Nombre _____

Hora _____

Fecha _____

**Guided Practice Activities 7B-3**

# The preterite of verbs ending in -*car* and -*gar* (p. 198)

- Verbs that end in **-car** and **-gar** use the same preterite endings as regular **-ar** verbs, except in the **yo** form.
- Here are the preterite forms of **buscar** (*to look for*) and **pagar** (*to pay*).

c → qu

| yo | **busqué** | nosotros/nosotras | **buscamos** |
|---|---|---|---|
| tú | **buscaste** | vosotros/vosotras | **buscasteis** |
| usted/él/ella | **buscó** | ustedes/ellos/ellas | **buscaron** |

g → gu

| yo | **pagué** | nosotros/nosotras | **pagamos** |
|---|---|---|---|
| tú | **pagaste** | vosotros/vosotras | **pagasteis** |
| usted/él/ella | **pagó** | ustedes/ellos/ellas | **pagaron** |

- Other verbs you know follow this pattern. **Jugar** is like **pagar** (g → gu). **Practicar, sacar**, and **tocar** are like **buscar** (c → qu).

**A.** Fill in the missing **yo** forms in the chart.

| | buscar | pagar | jugar | practicar | sacar | tocar |
|---|---|---|---|---|---|---|
| **yo** | | | | | | |
| **tú** | buscaste | pagaste | jugaste | practicaste | sacaste | tocaste |
| **Ud./él/ella** | buscó | pagó | jugó | practicó | sacó | tocó |
| **nosotros/nosotras** | buscamos | pagamos | jugamos | practicamos | sacamos | tocamos |
| **Uds./ellos/ellas** | buscaron | pagaron | jugaron | practicaron | sacaron | tocaron |

**B.** Write the correct forms of the verb indicated next to each subject pronoun. Follow the model.

Modelo   (pagar):  tú _____*pagaste*_____

1. (pagar): ellos _____
2. (pagar): yo _____
3. (pagar): él _____
4. (jugar): tú y yo _____
5. (jugar): yo _____
6. (jugar): Uds. _____
7. (buscar): ellos _____

8. (buscar): yo _____
9. (practicar): yo _____
10. (practicar): tú _____
11. (sacar): Ud. _____
12. (sacar): yo _____
13. (tocar): yo _____
14. (tocar): tú y yo _____

# Direct object pronouns (p. 202)

- A direct object tells who or what receives the action of the verb:

  **Busco una <u>cadena</u>.**     *I am looking for a <u>chain</u>.*

- In the sentence above, **cadena** is the direct object noun.

- You can use a direct object pronoun to replace a direct object noun.

- The direct object pronoun must match the noun it replaces in both gender and number:

  Compré <u>un suéter</u>.     → **Lo** compré. (*masculine, singular*)

  Compré <u>una falda</u>.     → **La** compré. (*feminine singular*)

  Compré <u>unos aretes</u>.    → **Los** compré. (*masculine plural*)

  Compré <u>unas pulseras</u>.   → **Las** compré. (*feminine plural*)

- The direct object comes *before* a verb in the present tense or the preterite tense.

  **Lo** tengo aquí. (*I have **it** here.*)

  **Lo** compré anoche. (*I bought **it** last night.*)

**A.** Underline the direct object noun in each sentence.

1. Busco unos guantes nuevos.
2. La dependienta vendió el perfume.
3. Compré dos llaveros.
4. Llevamos nuestras carteras.
5. Compramos un collar.
6. Miramos unas corbatas.
7. Buscaron una cadena.
8. Preparé el almuerzo.

**B.** Write each noun you circled in **part A** on the following lines. Write **M** or **F** next to the noun, depending on whether it is masculine or feminine. Then write **S** or **P** next to that, depending on whether the noun is singular or plural. Follow the model.

| Modelo | _guantes_   M, P |

1. _____ _____
2. _____ _____
3. _____ _____
4. _____ _____

5. _____ _____
6. _____ _____
7. _____ _____

**C.** Now, write the correct direct object pronoun to replace each noun you wrote in **part B.** Follow the model.

| Modelo | guantes, M, P: _____Los_____ busqué. |

1. _____ vendió.
2. _____ compré.
3. _____ llevamos.
4. _____ compramos.

5. _____ miramos.
6. _____ buscaron.
7. _____ preparé.

Go Online   WEB CODE jcd-0715
PHSchool.com

**Realidades B**

**Capítulo 7B**

Nombre _____

Hora _____

Fecha _____

**Guided Practice Activities 7B-5**

## Lectura: ¡De compras! (pp. 208–209)

**A.** The reading in your textbook is about shopping in Hispanic communities of four different U.S. cities: New York, Miami, Los Angeles, and San Antonio. Use what you know about each area of the country and make a list of three items you would expect to find in Hispanic shopping centers in each city.

1. New York
   a) _____
   b) _____
   c) _____

2. Miami
   a) _____
   b) _____
   c) _____

3. Los Angeles
   a) _____
   b) _____
   c) _____

4. San Antonio
   a) _____
   b) _____
   c) _____

**B.** Now, look at the descriptions from the reading in your textbook and decide which city is being described. Write the name of the city in the space provided. Each city will be used once.

1. _____ Hay bodegas que venden productos típicos cubanos.

2. _____ En las joyerías de la calle Olvera, venden joyas de plata: aretes, collares, anillos y mucho más.

3. _____ En la calle 116, venden ropa, comida típica del Caribe, discos compactos, libros y mucho más.

4. _____ Es esta ciudad bonita, hay tiendas de artesanías mexicanas que son fabulosas.

**C.** The narrator from the reading in your textbook buys things in each city. Some items may have been on your list in **part A**. Look at the things below that the narrator bought. Write the name of the city for each in the spaces provided.

1. _____ una piñata
2. _____ una camiseta con la bandera de Puerto Rico
3. _____ pasta de guayaba
4. _____ un sarape
5. _____ una pulsera bonita
6. _____ una blusa bordada

# Presentación escrita (p. 211)

**Task:** Write a letter to a cousin or other relative about a gift you bought for a member of your family. Let the relative know what you bought so that he or she will not buy the same item.

❶ **Prewrite.** Think of a birthday gift you bought for a family member's birthday. It could be current or in the past. Answer the following questions about the gift to help organize your thoughts. Use complete sentences when you answer.

    **1.** ¿Para quién es el regalo? _____

    **2.** ¿Qué compraste? _____

    **3.** ¿Dónde compraste el regalo? _____

    **4.** ¿Por qué compraste ese regalo? _____

    **5.** ¿Cuánto pagaste por el regalo? _____

❷ **Draft.** Use the form below to write a rough draft of your letter. Include all of the information you wrote in your answers in **part 1**. Look in your textbook for a model to help you.

Querido(a) _____ :
          *(name of the relative you are writing to)*

Compré _____ para _____ .

Lo compré en _____ .

Creo que _____ .

Pagué _____ .

Tu _____ ,
      *(your relationship to the person)*

_____
        *(your name)*

❸ **Revise.** Read your letter again before you give it to a partner to review. Your teacher will check:

   • how easy the letter is to understand

   • how much information is included about the gift

   • how appropriate the greeting and closing are

   • the accuracy of the use of the preterite

**Realidades B**

**Capítulo 8A**

Nombre _____

Fecha _____

Hora _____

**Vocabulary Flash Cards, Sheet 1**

Write the Spanish vocabulary word below each picture. If there is a word or phrase, copy it in the space provided. Be sure to include the article for each noun.

| la ciudad | el mar | el país |
|---|---|---|
| _____ | _____ | _____ |

| | | |
|---|---|---|
| _____ | _____ | _____ |

| | | |
|---|---|---|
| _____ | _____ | _____ |

Nombre _____

Hora _____

Fecha _____

**Vocabulary Flash Cards, Sheet 2**

el
animal

_____
_____

el
árbol

_____
_____

el
oso

_____
_____

la
atracción

_____
_____

| | | |
|---|---|---|
| **aprender (a)** | | **tomar el sol** |
| _____ __ | | _____ |
| **bucear** | **montar a caballo** | **visitar** |
| _____ | _____ ___ | _____ |
| **comprar recuerdos** | | **el lugar** |
| _____ | _____ | _____ |

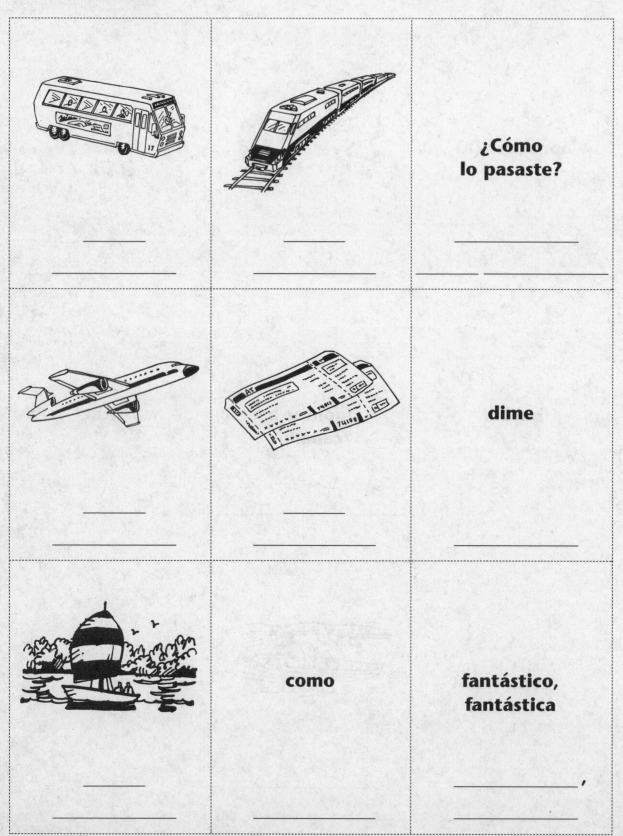

¿Cómo
lo pasaste?

_____

dime

como

fantástico,
fantástica

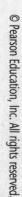

**Realidades** **B**

**Capítulo 8A**

Nombre _____

Hora _____

Fecha _____

**Vocabulary Flash Cards, Sheet 5**

| | | |
|---|---|---|
| **Fue un desastre.** <br><br> _____ <br> _____ | **ir de vacaciones** <br><br> ____ ____ <br> _____ | **¿Qué te pasó?** <br><br> _____ |
| **el hotel** <br><br> ____ <br> _____ | **Me gustó.** <br><br> _____ | **regresar** <br><br> _____ |
| **impresionante** <br><br> | **¿Qué hiciste?** <br><br> _____ | **salir** <br><br> _____ |

¿Te
gustó?

_____

_____

¿Viste...?

_____

durante

_____

tremendo,
tremenda

_____ ,

_____

viajar

_____

tarde

_____

vi

_____

el
viaje

_____

_____

temprano

_____

**Realidades B**

**Capítulo 8A**

Nombre _____

Hora _____

Fecha _____

**Vocabulary Check, Sheet 1**

Tear out this page. Write the English words on the lines. Fold the paper along the dotted line to see the correct answers so you can check your work.

la ciudad _____

el estadio _____

el lago _____

el mar _____

el monumento _____

el museo _____

el país _____

el parque de
diversiones _____
_____

el parque
nacional _____

la obra de
teatro _____

el zoológico _____

el árbol _____

el mono _____

el oso _____

el pájaro _____

aprender (a) _____

Fold In

**Realidades B**

**Capítulo 8A**

Nombre _____

Hora _____

Fecha _____

**Vocabulary Check, Sheet 2**

Tear out this page. Write the Spanish words on the lines. Fold the paper along the dotted line to see the correct answers so you can check your work.

city _____

stadium _____

lake _____

sea _____

monument _____

museum _____

country _____

amusement park _____
_____

national park _____
_____

play _____
_____

zoo _____

tree _____

monkey _____

bear _____

bird _____

to learn _____

Fold In

Tear out this page. Write the English words on the lines. Fold the paper along the dotted line to see the correct answers so you can check your work.

bucear _____

_____

recuerdos _____

descansar _____

montar a
caballo _____

_____

pasear en bote _____

tomar el sol _____

el autobús _____

el avión _____

el barco _____

el tren _____

ir de
vacaciones _____

_____

regresar _____

salir _____

_____

viajar _____

el viaje _____

Fold In

Tear out this page. Write the Spanish words on the lines. Fold the paper along the dotted line to see the correct answers so you can check your work.

to scuba dive/
snorkel                 _____

souvenirs               _____

to rest, to relax       _____

to ride
horseback               _____
                        _____

to go boating           _____

to sunbathe             _____

bus                     _____

airplane                _____

boat, ship              _____

train                   _____

to go on
vacation                _____
                        _____

to return               _____

to leave,
to get out              _____

to travel               _____

trip                    _____

To hear a complete list of the vocabulary for this chapter, go to Disc 2, Track 7 on the Guided Practice Audio CD, or go to www.phschool.com and type in the Web Code jcd-0889. Then click on **Repaso del capítulo.**

Fold In

**Realidades** **B**

**Capítulo 8A**

Nombre _____

Fecha _____

Hora _____

**Guided Practice Activities 8A-1**

# The preterite of *-er* and *-ir* verbs (p. 230)

- Regular **-er** and **-ir** verbs have their own set of preterite (past-tense) endings, just as they do in the present tense.
- The preterite endings for regular **-er** and **-ir** verbs are exactly the same.

| comer → com- + endings | | | |
|---|---|---|---|
| yo | comí | nosotros/nosotras | comimos |
| tú | comiste | vosotros/vosotras | comisteis |
| usted/él/ella | comió | ustedes/ellos/ellas | comieron |

| escribir → escrib- + endings | | | |
|---|---|---|---|
| yo | escribí | nosotros/nosotras | escribimos |
| tú | escribiste | vosotros/vosotras | escribisteis |
| usted/él/ella | escribió | ustedes/ellos/ellas | escribieron |

- Like regular **-ar** verbs in the preterite, regular **-er** and **-ir** verbs have an accent at the end of the **yo** and **usted/él/ella** forms: **comí, escribió.**

**A.** Write the missing preterite forms in the chart.

| | comer | escribir | aprender | salir | correr |
|---|---|---|---|---|---|
| **yo** | comí | | | | |
| **tú** | | escribiste | | | |
| **Ud./él/ella** | | | aprendió | | |
| **nosotros/nosotras** | | | | salimos | |
| **Uds./ellos/ellas** | | | | | corrieron |

**B.** Circle the correct preterite form to complete each sentence.

1. Sofía ( **comí** / **comió** ) en un restaurante mexicano.

2. Ellos ( **escribimos** / **escribieron** ) una tarjeta a sus abuelos.

3. Tú ( **aprendiste** / **aprendió** ) a hablar español.

4. Yo ( **salí** / **saliste** ) para el trabajo.

5. Tú y yo ( **corrieron** / **corrimos** ) en el parque anoche.

6. Marta y Marcos ( **comió** / **comieron** ) el almuerzo en la cafetería.

7. Yo ( **aprendí** / **aprendió** ) a montar en monopatín.

8. Usted ( **salió** / **salieron** ) después de las clases.

**Realidades B**

**Capítulo 8A**

Nombre _____

Hora _____

Fecha _____

**Guided Practice Activities 8A-2**

# The preterite of *-er* and *-ir* verbs *(continued)*

**C.** Complete the following sentences with the correct form of the verb in parentheses. Follow the model.

**Modelo**   Tú (**comer**) _____*comiste*_____ en la cafetería.

1. Nosotros (**escribir**) _____ unas tarjetas.

2. Tú (**aprender**) _____ a esquiar.

3. Yo (**correr**) _____ en el parque.

4. Ellos (**salir**) _____ de la escuela a las tres.

5. Ud. (**comer**) _____ una hamburguesa.

6. Nosotros (**ver**) _____ un video anoche.

7. Ustedes (**compartir**) _____ una pizza.

8. Tú y yo (**aprender**) _____ a montar en monopatín.

9. Yo (**vivir**) _____ en un apartamento.

10. Ella (**comprender**) _____ la lección de ayer.

**D.** Use verbs from the list to say what you and your friends did last week.

| | | | |
|---|---|---|---|
| aprender a | comer | compartir | escribir |
| ver | salir de | salir con | correr |

1. Yo _____ .

2. Yo no _____ .

3. Mis amigos y yo _____ .

4. Mis amigos y yo no _____ .

**Go Online** WEB CODE jcd-0803
PHSchool.com

# The preterite of *ir* (p. 232)

- **Ir** (*to go*) is an irregular verb in the present tense. It is also irregular in the preterite tense. Here are the preterite forms of **ir**.

| yo | **fui** | nosotros/nosotras | **fuimos** |
|---|---|---|---|
| tú | **fuiste** | vosotros/vosotras | **fuisteis** |
| usted/él/ella | **fue** | ustedes/ellos/ellas | **fueron** |

- The preterite forms of **ir** are the same as the preterite forms of the verb **ser** (*to be*). You can tell which verb is meant by the meaning of the sentence.

   Marcos **fue** a Nueva York.           *Marcos **went** to New York.*

   **Fue** un viaje fabuloso.              *It **was** a fabulous trip.*

**A.** Add the correct ending onto the preterite stem of **ir** to create its complete preterite form. Then rewrite the complete form. Follow the model.

Modelo     yo fu*i*___   _____*fui*_____

1. yo fu_____ _____      4. nosotros fu_____ _____

2. tú fu_____ _____      5. ellos fu_____ _____

3. ella fu_____ _____      6. ustedes fu_____ _____

**B.** Circle the correct form of **ir** to complete each sentence.

1. Yo ( **fue** / **fui** ) a la tienda de ropa.

2. Ellos ( **fueron** / **fuiste** ) al estadio de béisbol.

3. Tú ( **fueron** / **fuiste** ) a un parque nacional.

4. Nosotros ( **fuimos** / **fueron** ) al parque de diversiones.

5. Ud. ( **fui** / **fue** ) al teatro.

6. Uds. ( **fuiste** / **fueron** ) a la ciudad para comprar ropa.

7. Tú y yo ( **fuimos** / **fuiste** ) al mar para bucear.

**C.** Complete each sentence by writing in the correct form of **ir**.

1. Yo _____ a un lugar muy bonito.

2. Tú _____ al estadio de fútbol americano.

3. Ella _____ al lago para pasear en bote.

4. Nosotros _____ a la playa para tomar el sol.

5. Ellos _____ al teatro para ver una obra de teatro.

6. Ud. _____ al monumento en el parque nacional.

**Go Online** WEB CODE jcd-0804
PHSchool.com

**Realidades B**

**Capítulo 8A**

Nombre _____

Hora _____

Fecha _____

**Guided Practice Activities 8A-4**

# The personal *a* (p. 236)

- You have learned to identify the direct object of a sentence. The direct object tells who or what receives the action of the verb.

  Compré <u>un anillo</u>.    *I bought <u>a ring</u>.*

  Vi <u>una obra de teatro</u>.    *I saw <u>a play</u>.*

- When the direct object is a person, a group of people, or a pet, you use **a** in front of the direct object. This use of the personal **a** has no equivalent in English and is not translated.

  Vi <u>un video</u>.    *I saw <u>a video</u>.*

  Vi **a** <u>mi abuela</u>.    *I saw <u>my grandmother</u>.*

  Vi **a** <u>mi perro León</u>.    *I saw <u>my dog León</u>.*

**A.** Underline the direct object in each sentence.

**1.** Vi un video.

**2.** Escribo una carta.

**3.** Visitaron a su familia.

**4.** Comimos una pizza.

**5.** Compraste una corbata.

**6.** Buscamos a nuestro perro.

**B.** Now, go look at each sentence from **part A** and write **P** next to those that refer to people or pets.

**1.** Vi un video. _____

**2.** Escribo una carta. _____

**3.** Visitaron a su familia. _____

**4.** Comimos una pizza. _____

**5.** Compraste una corbata. _____

**6.** Buscamos a nuestro perro. _____

**C.** Look at the sentences above in **part B** that you labeled with a **P**. Circle the personal **a** in each of those sentences.

**D.** Look at each sentence. If it requires a personal **a**, circle the **a** in parentheses. If it does not require a personal **a**, cross out the **a** in parentheses.

**1.** Compramos ( a ) un traje de baño y unos anteojos de sol.

**2.** Yo vi ( a ) un monumento grande en el parque nacional.

**3.** Escribimos muchas tarjetas ( a ) nuestros primos.

**4.** Visité ( a ) mi familia durante las vacaciones.

**5.** Lavaron ( a ) su perro Fifí.

**6.** Buscamos ( a ) una tienda de ropa buena.

**7.** Compré ( a ) un boleto de avión ayer.

**8.** Busqué ( a ) mi hermano menor en el parque de atracciones.

Go Online WEB CODE jcd-0805
PHSchool.com

**Realidades B**

**Capítulo 8A**

Nombre _____

Fecha _____

Hora _____

**Guided Practice Activities 8A-5**

## Lectura: Álbum de mi viaje a Perú (pp. 240–241)

**A.** Sometimes you can use clues from the context of what you are reading to help discover the meaning of the word. Try to find the meaning of the five words listed below by using context clues from the reading in your textbook. Write in the English equivalent of each word in the space provided.

1. antigua _____

2. impresionantes _____

3. altura _____

4. construyeron _____

5. nivel _____

**B.** The reading in your textbook is a journal entry from a trip to Perú by the author Sofía Porrúa. Each day that she writes in the journal, she is in a different location. Choose the location from the word bank and write it next to the day to which it corresponds.

| Cuzco | Machu Picchu | sobre las líneas de Nazca | en el lago Titicaca | Lima |
| --- | --- | --- | --- | --- |

1. domingo, 25 de julio _____

2. miércoles, 28 de julio _____

3. jueves, 29 de julio _____

4. sábado, 31 de julio _____

5. miércoles, 4 de agosto _____

**C.** In the first log entry, Sofía mentions her two companions, Beto and Carmen. Read the passage below about these two friends and answer the questions that follow.

*Beto está sacando muchas fotos con su cámara digital. Carmen está dibujando todo lo que ve. Las montañas son fantásticas.*

1. Sofía is capturing the trip by keeping a journal. How is Beto capturing the trip?

_____ And Carmen? _____

2. What is Beto using to capture the trip? _____

What do you think Carmen is using? _____

# Presentación oral (p. 243)

**Task:** You will talk about a trip you took. It can be a real or an imaginary trip. Use photographs or drawings to make your talk more interesting.

**A.** Think about the specifics of your trip. Answer the questions below in Spanish with as much detail as you can think of. Use complete sentences.

1. ¿Cuándo fuiste de viaje? _____

_____

2. ¿Qué hiciste en tu viaje? _____

_____

3. ¿Qué lugares visitaste? _____

_____

4. ¿A quiénes viste? _____

_____

5. ¿Compraste algo? _____ ¿Qué compraste? _____

_____

**B.** You will need to create a visual presentation to go along with your talk. You can bring in actual photos or you can create drawings of a trip. Organize and attach your drawings or photos to a piece of posterboard. A good way to do this would be to put them in order of when they happened, going from the top to the bottom of the page.

**C.** Read the following model before you write up the script for your talk. Notice that you should add how you felt about the trip at the end.

> *En marzo de este año, fui a Florida para visitar a mi abuelita y a mis primos. Tomamos el sol en la playa y nadamos mucho. Aprendí a bucear y vi animales muy interesantes en el mar. Me gusta mucho Florida. Es un lugar fantástico. El viaje fue muy divertido.*

**D.** Now, write what you are going to say about your trip on the lines below. Remember to refer back to your photos or drawings.

_____

_____

_____

_____

**Realidades** **B**

**Capítulo 8B**

Nombre _____

Fecha _____

Hora _____

**Vocabulary Flash Cards, Sheet 1**

Write the Spanish vocabulary word below each picture. If there is a word or phrase, copy it in the space provided. Be sure to include the article for each noun.

| | | |
|---|---|---|
| _____ _____ | _____ _____ | _____ _____ |
| _____ _____ | _____ _____ | _____ _____ |
| _____ _____ | _____ _____ | _____ _____ |

**llevar**

_____

**usado,
usada**

_____ ,

_____

_____

_____

**recoger**

_____

**reciclar**

_____

**la
comunidad**

_____

_____

**separar**

_____

**el
barrio**

_____

_____

**Realidades** **B**

**Capítulo 8B**

Nombre _____

Fecha _____

Hora _____

**Vocabulary Flash Cards, Sheet 4**

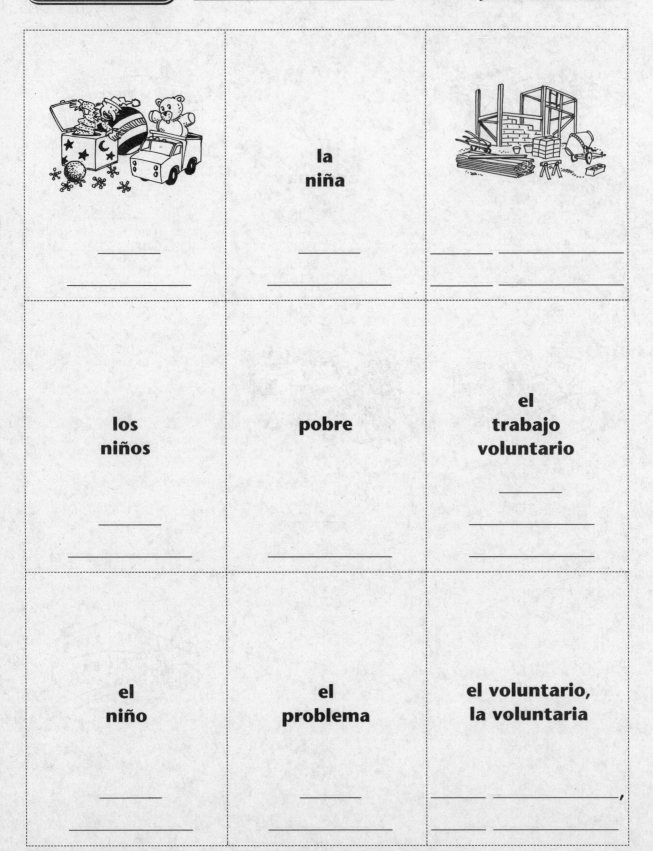

la
niña

_____

_____

_____

_____

los
niños

_____

_____

pobre

_____

el
trabajo
voluntario

_____

_____

el
niño

_____

_____

el
problema

_____

_____

el voluntario,
la voluntaria

_____ _____ ,

_____ _____

**Realidades B**

**Capítulo 8B**

Nombre _____

Hora _____

Fecha _____

**Vocabulary Flash Cards, Sheet 5**

| | | |
|---|---|---|
| **a menudo** _____ _____ | **la experiencia** _____ _____ | **inolvidable** _____ _____ |
| **decidir** _____ | **Hay que...** _____ | **¿Qué más?** _____ _____ |
| **Es necesario.** _____ _____ | **increíble** _____ _____ | **la vez** _____ _____ |

Nombre _____    Hora _____

Fecha _____    **Vocabulary Flash Cards, Sheet 6**

otra
vez

_____
_____

_____

_____

decir

_____

_____

_____

_____

_____

_____

_____

_____

_____

Nombre _____

Fecha _____

Hora _____

Tear out this page. Write the English words on the lines. Fold the paper along the dotted line to see the correct answers so you can check your work.

la bolsa _____

la botella _____

la caja _____

el cartón _____

el centro de reciclaje _____
_____

la lata _____

llevar _____
_____

el periódico _____

el plástico _____

reciclar _____

recoger _____
_____

separar _____

usado, usada _____

el vidrio _____

el barrio _____

la calle _____

la comunidad _____

Fold In

**Realidades** B

Nombre _____

Hora _____

**Capítulo 8B**

Fecha _____

**Vocabulary Check, Sheet 2**

Tear out this page. Write the Spanish words on the lines. Fold the paper along the dotted line to see the correct answers so you can check your work.

bag, sack _____

bottle _____

box _____

cardboard _____

recycling
center _____

_____

can _____

to take;
to carry _____

newspaper _____

plastic _____

to recycle _____

to collect;
to gather _____

to separate _____

used _____

glass _____

neighborhood _____

street, road _____

community _____

Fold In

**Realidades B**

**Capítulo 8B**

Nombre _____

Fecha _____

Hora _____

**Vocabulary Check, Sheet 3**

Tear out this page. Write the English words on the lines. Fold the paper along the dotted line to see the correct answers so you can check your work.

el jardín                    _____

el río                       _____

los ancianos                 _____

el campamento                _____

los demás                    _____

la escuela primaria          _____

la gente                     _____

el juguete                   _____

los niños                    _____

pobre                        _____

el proyecto de               _____
construcción                 _____

el trabajo                   _____
voluntario

Fold In

Tear out this page. Write the Spanish words on the lines. Fold the paper along the dotted line to see the correct answers so you can check your work.

garden, yard _____

river _____

older people _____

camp _____

others _____

primary school _____

people _____

toy _____

children _____

poor _____

construction project _____

volunteer work _____

_____

Fold In

To hear a complete list of the vocabulary for this chapter, go to Disc 2, Track 8 on the Guided Practice Audio CD, or go to www.phschool.com and type in the Web Code jcd-0899. Then click on **Repaso del capítulo.**

# The present tense of *decir* (p. 262)

- **Decir** (*to say, to tell*) is irregular in the present tense. Here are its forms:

| yo | **digo** | nosotros/nosotras | **decimos** |
|---|---|---|---|
| tú | **dices** | vosotros/vosotras | **decís** |
| usted/él/ella | **dice** | ustedes/ellos/ellas | **dicen** |

- Notice that all the forms have an **i** in the stem except for the **nosotros/nosotras** and **vosotros/vosotras** forms (**decimos, decís**).

**A.** Write the correct forms of **decir** in the chart.

| yo | nosotros/nosotras | |
|---|---|---|
| tú | vosotros/vosotras | decís |
| Ud./él/ella | Uds./ellos/ellas | |

**B.** Circle the correct forms of **decir** to complete each sentence.

1. Mis abuelos ( **dicen** / **dice** ) que el parque es bonito.

2. Yo ( **dices** / **digo** ) que es un video interesante.

3. Tú ( **dices** / **dicen** ) que el restaurante es bueno.

4. Ellos ( **dice** / **dicen** ) que la profesora es inteligente.

5. Nosotros ( **dicen** / **decimos** ) que el parque de diversiones es fantástico.

6. Ustedes ( **digo** / **dicen** ) que es divertido bucear.

7. Tú y yo ( **dices** / **decimos** ) que nos gusta pasear en bote.

**C.** Write complete sentences to find out what the people indicated say about a museum. Follow the model.

Modelo   Inés / decir que es fantástico

          *Inés dice que es fantástico.*

1. tú / decir que es aburrido _____

2. yo / decir que es interesante _____

3. ellos / decir que es divertido _____

4. nosotros / decir que es grande _____

5. Ud. / decir que es impresionante _____

# Indirect object pronouns (p. 264)

- An indirect object tells to whom or for whom an action is performed. In order to identify an indirect object, take the verb in the sentence and ask "For whom?" or "To whom?"

  **Te** traigo un recuerdo.                    *I bring **you** a souvenir.*

  *"To whom do I bring a souvenir?"*        *"To **you**."*

- Indirect object pronouns must agree with the person they refer to.

|  | Singular |  | Plural |
|---|---|---|---|
| **(yo)** | **me** (to/for) me | **(nosotros)** | **nos** (to/for) us |
| **(tú)** | **te** (to/for) you (familiar) |  |  |
| **(Ud./él/ella)** | **le** (to/for) you (formal), him, her | **(Uds./ellos/ellas)** | **les** (to/for) you (formal), them |

- Like direct object pronouns, indirect object pronouns go before a conjugated verb.

  **Te** compré una tarjeta.                    *I bought **you** a card.*

- When there is an infinitive with a conjugated verb, the indirect object pronoun can attach to the end of the infinitive or go before the conjugated verb.

  **Me** van a comprar una camiseta.        *They are going to buy **me** a T-shirt.*

  Van a comprar**me** una camiseta.          *They are going to buy **me** a T-shirt.*

**A.** Underline the indirect object pronoun in each sentence.

1. Te escribí una tarjeta.                4. Nos dan regalos.

2. Me trae un vaso de agua.              5. Les compramos una camiseta.

3. Le ayudo con la tarea.                6. Le llevamos unos libros.

**B.** Circle the correct indirect object pronoun. Follow the model.

**Modelo**   tú:     ( (**Te**) / **Le** ) damos un boleto de avión.

1. yo:          ( **Me** / **Nos** ) ayudan con la tarea.

2. tú:          ( **Te** / **Les** ) llevo un regalo.

3. ella:        ( **Le** / **Les** ) escribo una tarjeta.

4. nosotros:    ( **Nos** / **Les** ) compraron unos zapatos.

5. ellos:       ( **Le** / **Les** ) trae un vaso de agua.

6. él:          ( **Le** / **Me** ) lavo el coche.

7. tú:          ( **Me** / **Te** ) damos unas flores.

8. tú y yo:     ( **Me** / **Nos** ) traen un recuerdo de las vacaciones.

**Go Online**  WEB CODE jcd-0815
**PHSchool.com**

# Indirect object pronouns (continued)

**C.** Write the correct indirect object pronoun in each sentence. Follow the model.

**Modelo**   yo: _____*Me*_____ traen el periódico.

   **1.** yo: _____ ayudan a limpiar el baño.

   **2.** tú: _____ compran una sudadera.

   **3.** él: _____ dan una bicicleta nueva.

   **4.** nosotros: _____ traen unas cajas de cartón.

   **5.** Ud.: _____ escriben una tarjeta.

   **6.** ellos: _____ compro unos platos.

   **7.** tú y yo: _____ traen una pizza grande.

   **8.** Uds.: _____ compro un boleto de avión.

   **9.** yo: _____ traen un vaso de jugo.

   **10.** tú: _____ dan unos juguetes.

**D.** Write sentences to say to whom Susana is telling the truth. Follow the model.

**Modelo**   yo   *Susana me dice la verdad.*

   **1.** tú _____

   **2.** él _____

   **3.** nosotros _____

   **4.** ellos _____

   **5.** ella _____

   **6.** tú y yo _____

   **7.** ustedes _____

# The preterite of *hacer* and *dar* (p. 266)

- The verbs **hacer** (*to make, to do*) and **dar** (*to give*) are irregular in the preterite.

**hacer**

| yo | **hice** | nosotros/nosotras | **hicimos** |
|---|---|---|---|
| tú | **hiciste** | vosotros/vosotras | **hicisteis** |
| usted/él/ella | **hizo** | ustedes/ellos/ellas | **hicieron** |

**dar**

| yo | **di** | nosotros/nosotras | **dimos** |
|---|---|---|---|
| tú | **diste** | vosotros/vosotras | **disteis** |
| usted/él/ella | **dio** | ustedes/ellos/ellas | **dieron** |

- These verbs have no accent marks in the preterite forms.
- Notice the change from **c** to **z** in the **usted/él/ella** form of **hacer: hizo**.

**A.** Write the missing forms of **hacer** and **dar** in the chart.

|  | hacer | dar |
|---|---|---|
| **yo** | hice | |
| **tú** | | diste |
| **Ud./él/ella** | | dio |
| **nosotros/nosotras** | hicimos | |
| **Uds./ellos/ellas** | | dieron |

**B.** Circle the correct forms of **hacer** and **dar** for each subject pronoun.

1. tú ( **diste** / **dio** ), ( **hizo** / **hiciste** )
2. yo ( **dio** / **di** ), ( **hice** / **hicimos** )
3. tú y yo ( **dimos** / **diste** ), ( **hizo** / **hicimos** )
4. ellas ( **di** / **dieron** ), ( **hice** / **hicieron** )
5. él ( **diste** / **dio** ), ( **hizo** / **hice** )
6. Ud. ( **di** / **dio** ), ( **hizo** / **hiciste** )

**C.** Complete each sentence with the correct form of the verb indicated. Follow the model. The boldfaced word is the subject of the sentence.

Modelo   **Ella** me (dar) _____*dio*_____ un libro.

1. **Tú** me (dar) _____ un regalo bonito.
2. **Ellos** me (hacer) _____ un suéter fantástico.
3. **Nosotros** te (dar) _____ unos discos compactos.
4. **Ud.** me (hacer) _____ un pastel sabroso.

Go Online WEB CODE jcd-0814
PHSchool.com

**Realidades B**

**Capítulo 8B**

Nombre _____

Hora _____

Fecha _____

**Guided Practice Activities 8B-5**

# Lectura: Hábitat para la Humanidad Internacional (pp. 272–273)

**A.** Recognizing cognates has helped you understand many of the readings in your textbook. The reading on Habitat for Humanity is no exception. Look at the words below and write their English equivalents in the spaces provided.

1. organización _____

2. internacional _____

3. comunidades _____

4. donaciones _____

5. privadas _____

6. miembros _____

**B.** Answer the following questions in Spanish in order to understand the main idea of the reading in your textbook.

1. ¿Qué es Hábitat y qué hace? Hábitat es una _____

_____ .

2. ¿Cuál es el objetivo de Hábitat? Su objetivo es _____

_____ .

3. ¿Cuántos proyectos en total tiene Hábitat en el mundo? Hábitat tiene _____

_____ .

**C.** Now, read the following passage to get more specific information about a typical Habitat project. Answer the questions that follow.

> *Según Hábitat, las personas pobres tienen que ayudar a construir sus casas. Es una manera positiva de ayudar a los demás. Hábitat les da los materiales de construcción y los trabajadores voluntarios.*

1. According to Habitat, who has to help build the houses? _____

_____

2. Who gives these people materials? _____

_____

3. Who else helps build the houses? _____

_____

4. Why do you think Habitat has such success? _____

_____

_____

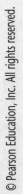

**Realidades** (B)

**Capítulo 8B**

Nombre _____

Hora _____

Fecha _____

**Guided Practice Activities 8B-6**

# Presentación escrita (p. 275)

**Task:** Imagine that you have to organize a clean-up campaign for a park, recreation center, school playground, or other place in your community. Make a poster announcing the project and inviting students to participate.

❶ **Prewrite.** Answer the following questions about your project:

a) ¿Qué van a limpiar ustedes?

_____

b) ¿Dónde está el lugar?

_____

c) ¿Qué tienen que hacer para preparar a limpiar?

_____

d) ¿Qué día van a trabajar?

_____

e) ¿Cuántas horas van a trabajar?

_____

f) ¿Quién(es) puede(n) participar?

_____

❷ **Draft.** Your answers to the questions above will determine what you say in your rough draft. Write your answers on a separate sheet of paper and organize them so that they will be easy to read and understand. You should also include any drawings, photos, or useful magazine cutouts you can find as part of your poster.

❸ **Revise.** Check your rough draft to make sure it is what you want. Your partner will check your work. Look on page 419 of your textbook to see what he or she will check.

❹ **Publish.** Take your partner's suggestions and do the changes necessary to make your poster as complete and effective as you can. Since you are now working on your final draft, your writing should be neat and your presentation should be on a clean poster. Your work may be presented in the classroom or even on the walls elsewhere in school, so make it look attractive!

Nombre _____

Hora _____

Fecha _____

Write the Spanish vocabulary word below each picture. If there is a word or phrase, copy it in the space provided. Be sure to include the article for each noun.

**el canal**

_____

_____

_____

_____

_____

_____

_____

_____

_____

_____

_____

_____

_____

_____

_____

_____

_____

_____

_____

_____

_____

_____

_____

_____

_____

_____

_____   _____

_____

_____

_____

_____

_____

_____

**la**

**actriz**

_____

_____

**Realidades B**

**Capítulo 9A**

Nombre _____

Fecha _____

Hora _____

**Vocabulary Flash Cards, Sheet 3**

**cómico, cómica**

_____,

_____

**infantil**

_____

**violento, violenta**

_____,

_____

**emocionante**

_____

**realista**

_____

**me aburre(n)**

_____

**fascinante**

_____

**tonto, tonta**

_____,

_____

**me interesa(n)**

_____

_____

**Realidades B**

**Capítulo 9A**

Nombre _____

Hora _____

Fecha _____

**Vocabulary Flash Cards, Sheet 4**

dar

_____

terminar

_____

medio,
media

_____,

_____

durar

_____

más de

_____

¿Qué clase
de...?

_____ _____

_____

empezar

_____

menos de

_____

acabar de

_____

**Realidades B**

**Capítulo 9A**

Nombre _____

Hora _____

Fecha _____

**Vocabulary Flash Cards, Sheet 5**

aburrir

_____

faltar

_____

antes de

_____

doler

_____

interesar

_____

casi

_____

encantar

_____

quedar

_____

¿De veras?

_____

**Realidades** **B**

**Capítulo 9A**

Nombre _____

Fecha _____

Hora _____

**Vocabulary Flash Cards, Sheet 6**

especialmente

_____

ya

_____

_____

por eso

_____

_____

_____

_____

_____

_____

sobre

_____

_____

_____

_____

**Realidades B**

**Capítulo 9A**

Nombre _____

Hora _____

Fecha _____

**Vocabulary Check, Sheet 1**

Tear out this page. Write the English words on the lines. Fold the paper along the dotted line to see the correct answers so you can check your work.

el canal _____

el programa
de concursos _____

el programa de
dibujos animados _____

el programa
deportivo _____

el programa de
entrevistas _____

el programa de
la vida real _____

el programa de
noticias _____

el programa
educativo _____
_____

el programa
musical _____
_____

la telenovela _____

la comedia _____

el drama _____

la película de
ciencia ficción _____
_____

Fold In
←

Tear out this page. Write the Spanish words on the lines. Fold the paper along the dotted line to see the correct answers so you can check your work.

channel _____

game show _____

_____

cartoon show _____

_____

sports show _____

_____

interview show _____

_____

reality program _____

_____

news program _____

_____

educational program _____

_____

musical program _____

_____

soap opera _____

comedy _____

drama _____

science fiction movie _____

_____

Fold In →

**Realidades** **B**

**Capítulo 9A**

Nombre _____

Hora _____

Fecha _____

**Vocabulary Check, Sheet 3**

Tear out this page. Write the English words on the lines. Fold the paper along the dotted line to see the correct answers so you can check your work.

la película de
horror                  _____

la película
policíaca               _____

                        _____

la película
romántica               _____

                        _____

emocionante             _____

fascinante              _____

infantil                _____

                        _____

tonto, tonta            _____

violento, violenta      _____

el actor                _____

la actriz               _____

dar                     _____

durar                   _____

empezar                 _____

terminar                _____

Fold In

Nombre _____     Hora _____

Fecha _____     **Vocabulary Check, Sheet 4**

Tear out this page. Write the Spanish words on the lines. Fold the paper along the dotted line to see the correct answers so you can check your work.

horror movie                    _____

_____

crime movie,                    _____
mystery
_____

romantic                        _____
movie
_____

touching                        _____

fascinating                     _____

for children;                   _____
childish

silly, stupid                   _____

violent                         _____

actor                           _____

actress                         _____

to show                         _____

to last                         _____

to begin                        _____

to end                          _____

To hear a complete list of the vocabulary for this chapter, go to Disc 2, Track 9 on the Guided Practice Audio CD, or go to www.phschool.com and type in the Web Code jcd-0989. Then click on **Repaso del capítulo.**

Fold In →

## *Acabar de* + infinitive (p. 294)

- Use present-tense forms of **acabar** with an infinitive to say that you and others have just finished doing something.

| | |
|---|---|
| **Acabo de tomar** una siesta. | *I just took a nap.* |
| **Acabamos de patinar.** | *We just went skating.* |

- Here are the present-tense forms of **acabar**, which is a regular **-ar** verb.

| yo | acabo | nosotros/nosotras | acabamos |
|---|---|---|---|
| tú | acabas | vosotros/vosotras | acabáis |
| usted/él/ella | acaba | ustedes/ellos/ellas | acaban |

**A.** Write the correct forms of **acabar** in the chart.

| yo | nosotros/nosotras | |
|---|---|---|
| tú | vosotros/vosotras | acabáis |
| Ud./él/ella | Uds./ellos/ellas | |

**B.** Circle the correct form of **acabar** to complete each sentence.

1. Yo ( **acaba** / **acabo** ) de ver un programa de la vida real.

2. Tú ( **acabas** / **acabamos** ) de ir al cine.

3. Ellos ( **acaban** / **acaba** ) de ver un video.

4. Tú y yo ( **acabas** / **acabamos** ) de cambiar el canal.

5. Usted ( **acabo** / **acaba** ) de ver una película policíaca.

6. Nosotros ( **acabas** / **acabamos** ) de hablar de las comedias.

7. Ustedes ( **acabamos** / **acaban** ) de comprar un lector DVD.

**C.** Complete each sentence with an activity you recently finished. Use the activities from **part B** above for ideas.

1. Yo acabo de _____.

2. Mis amigos y yo acabamos de _____.

3. Mi profesor (profesora) acaba de _____.

4. Los estudiantes de la escuela acaban de _____.

**Realidades B**

**Capítulo 9A**

Nombre _____

Fecha _____

Hora _____

**Guided Practice Activities 9A-2**

## *Acabar de* + infinitive *(continued)*

**D.** Complete the following conversations with the correct forms of **acabar**.

ADELA:   Mis amigos y yo _____ de ver una película de horror.

ANA:   ¿Sí? ¡Qué casualidad! Yo también _____ de ver una película de horror.

LUIS:   ¿Tú _____ de ver las noticias?

MARCOS:   Sí. ¿Y ustedes?

LUIS:   Nosotros _____ de ver un programa de concursos.

**E.** Create complete sentences. Follow the model.

Modelo   Alejandra / acabar de / sacar la basura

_Alejandra acaba de sacar la basura._ _____

**1.** Natalia / acabar de / dar de comer al gato

_____

**2.** yo / acabar de / lavar los platos

_____

**3.** ellos / acabar de / quitar la mesa

_____

**4.** tú y yo / acabar de / cortar el césped

_____

**5.** tú / acabar de / limpiar el baño

_____

**6.** Ud. / acabar de / pasar la aspiradora

_____

**F.** Complete each sentence with forms of **acabar de** to say what you and other people you know recently did.

**1.** Yo _____.

**2.** Mi familia _____.

**3.** Mis amigos y yo _____.

**4.** Los estudiantes de la escuela _____.

**Go Online** WEB CODE jcd-0903
PHSchool.com

**Realidades B**

**Capítulo 9A**

Nombre _____

Fecha _____

Hora _____

**Guided Practice Activities 9A-3**

# *Gustar* and similar verbs (p. 296)

- **Gustar** (*to please*) is different from other verbs you've learned. It is only used in its *third person forms*: **gusta** and **gustan**.
- **Gustar** is used with *indirect object pronouns* (**me, te, le, nos,** and **les**).
- **Gustar** agrees with the *subject* of the sentence, which is the object or objects that are pleasing to someone.

    indirect object pronoun + <u>**gusta**</u> + <u>singular</u> subject:

    Me **gusta** esa **comedia**.  *I like that comedy. (That comedy pleases me.)*

    indirect object pronoun + <u>**gustan**</u> + <u>plural</u> subject:

    Nos **gusta<u>n</u>** los **drama<u>s</u>**.  *We like dramas. (Dramas please us.)*

- Some other verbs are similar to **gustar**:

    **aburrir (aburre/aburren)** *(to bore)*:        Me **aburre** ese **programa**.

    Me **aburren** las **telenovelas**.

    **doler (duele/duelen)** *(to hurt)*:            Te **duele** la **mano**.

    Te **duelen** los **pies**.

    **encantar (encanta/encantan)** *(to like a lot)*:   Nos **encanta** el **teatro**.

    Nos **encantan** los **museos**.

    **faltar (falta/faltan)** *(to lack, to be missing)*:   Les **falta** un **vaso**.

    Les **faltan** los **anteojos**.

    **interesar (interesa/interesan)** *(to interest)*:   Me **interesa** la **literatura**.

    Me **interesan** las **ciencias**.

    **quedar (queda/quedan)** *(to fit)*:            Te **queda** bien el **vestido**.

    Te **quedan** bien los **zapatos**.

**A.** Look at each sentence. Circle the subject and underline the form of **gustar**. Follow the model.

Modelo    Te <u>gustan</u> los (programas) de noticias.   *P*

1. Me gustan los programas de entrevista.  _____

2. Nos gusta la telenovela nueva.  _____

3. ¿Te gusta el canal de deportes?  _____

4. Les gustan los programas de dibujos animados.  _____

5. Le gustan los programas de la vida real.  _____

6. Nos gusta el programa musical en el canal 27.  _____

**B.** Now, go back to the sentences in **part A** and write an **S** if they are singular (**gusta** + singular subject) or a **P** if they are plural (**gustan** + plural subject).

# *Gustar* and similar verbs (*continued*)

**C.** Circle the correct form of **gustar** to complete each sentence.

1. Nos ( **gusta** / **gustan** ) las ciudades grandes.

2. Te ( **gusta** / **gustan** ) los parques nacionales.

3. Les ( **gusta** / **gustan** ) el teatro.

4. Me ( **gusta** / **gustan** ) el parque de diversiones.

5. Le ( **gusta** / **gustan** ) los animales.

**D.** Write the correct form of **gustar** to complete each sentence.

1. Nos _____ los jeans.  4. Me _____ el traje.

2. Les _____ los zapatos.  5. Te _____ las botas.

3. Le _____ la gorra.  6. Les _____ el suéter.

**E.** These sentences use verbs that are similar to **gustar**. Circle the correct form for each verb.

1. Nos ( **encanta** / **encantan** ) las tiendas de ropa.

2. Me ( **aburre** / **aburren** ) los programas de la vida real.

3. Te ( **duele** / **duelen** ) los pies.

4. Les ( **interesa** / **interesan** ) los programas de noticias.

5. Le ( **falta** / **faltan** ) un cuchillo.

6. Me ( **queda** / **quedan** ) bien la falda.

**F.** Now write **a** or **an** to complete each of the following verbs.

1. Me encant_____ los programas de concursos.

2. Te interes_____ la nueva telenovela.

3. Nos falt_____ un vaso.

4. Me qued_____ bien la sudadera.

**G.** Write **e** or **en** to complete each of the following verbs.

1. Le aburr_____ los programas educativos.

2. Me duel_____ la cabeza.

3. Nos aburr_____ ese libro.

4. Te duel_____ el estómago.

**Go Online** WEB CODE jcd-0904
**PHSchool.com**

**Realidades B**

**Capítulo 9A**

Nombre _____

Fecha _____

Hora _____

**Guided Practice Activities 9A-5**

## Lectura: Una semana sin televisión (pp. 300–301)

**A.** Read through the reading in your textbook without stopping to look up words in a dictionary. On a separate sheet of paper, make a list of any words you don't know. Then, answer the following questions about the reading in Spanish. If you have trouble with any of the words, look them up while you answer the questions.

**1.** ¿Qué dos cosas hacen los niños estadounidenses más que cualquier otra cosa?

_____ y _____

**2.** ¿Según los estudios, ¿cuáles son tres resultados malos del ver demasiado la television?

_____, _____ y

_____

**3.** ¿Qué hacen millones de personas durante el mes de abril?

_____.

**B.** Read through the reading in your textbook once more. If there are words or phrases you still do not understand, look them up in a dictionary. Now, answer the questions below circling **C** for **cierto** (*true*) and **F** for **falso** (*false*).

**1.** C F   Según la lectura, los niños comen más que cualquier otra cosa, a excepción de dormir.

**2.** C F   Ver demasiado la televisión puede resultar en un exceso de peso.

**3.** C F   En cuatro horas de dibujos animados el sábado por la mañana, los niños pueden ver más de 200 anuncios sobre los deportes.

**4.** C F   Hay estudios que dicen que los niños que ven demasiado la tele pueden tener más probabilidad de ser violentos y agresivos de adultos.

**5.** C F   Para muchas familias en varios países una semana sin televisión les da la oportunidad de hacer cosas interesantes en vez de ver la tele.

**C.** You may have a discussion about the benefits and drawbacks of watching TV. Think of which argument you want to support. Then write three reasons in Spanish for why you feel this way. You can use information from the reading in your textbook or from personal experience.

**Razón 1:** _____

**Razón 2:** _____

**Razón 3:** _____

WEB CODE jcd-0905
PHSchool.com

**Realidades** **B**

**Capítulo 9A**

Nombre _____

Fecha _____

Hora _____

**Guided Practice Activities 9A-6**

# Presentación oral (p. 303)

**Task:** You are going to write a review of a movie or television show that was on your school's closed-circuit TV system. Prepare a summary of the movie or show.

**A.** Choose a movie or show to talk about. Fill in the chart with the information about your show or movie.

| | |
|---|---|
| Nombre | |
| Clase de película o programa | |
| Actor/Actores | |
| Actriz/Actrices | |
| Cómo es | |
| Cuánto tiempo dura | |
| Para quiénes es | |

**B.** Collect visuals to go along with your presentation. They could be ads or photos from a newspaper or magazine, such as a TV guide, or you could download pictures from the Internet. Make a poster with all of the items you collect.

**C.** Use the notes you took in **part A** to prepare your presentation. Write out complete sentences for each topic in the spaces below.

1. _____ .
2. _____ .
3. _____ .
4. _____ .
5. _____ .
6. _____ .
7. _____ .

**D.** Now, put together your finished poster and your sentences and practice your presentation. Remember to:

_____ speak clearly

_____ use complete sentences

_____ provide all key information about the movie or show

Realidades **B**

Capítulo 9B

Nombre

Hora

Fecha

**Vocabulary Flash Cards, Sheet 1**

Write the Spanish vocabulary word below each picture. If there is a word or phrase, copy it in the space provided. Be sure to include the article for each noun.

| | | |
|---|---|---|
| | **enviar** | **buscar** |
| | | |
| **comunicarse** | **bajar** | **la canción** |

| | | |
|---|---|---|
| **la composición** _____ _____ | **el curso** _____ _____ | **el documento** _____ _____ |
| _____ _____ | _____ _____ | **escribir por correo electrónico** _____ _____ _____ |
| **crear** _____ _____ | _____ _____ | **estar en línea** _____ _____ |

el
informe

los
gráficos

el
laboratorio

la
presentación

la
información

| | | |
|---|---|---|
| **visitar salones de chat**<br><br>_____<br><br>_____<br><br>_____ | **¿Qué te parece?**<br><br>_____ ___ | **tener miedo (de)**<br><br>_____ ___ |
| **complicado, complicada**<br><br>_____,<br><br>_____ | **rápidamente**<br><br>_____ | **conocer**<br><br>_____ |
| **¿Para qué sirve?**<br><br>_____<br><br>_____ | **Sirve para...**<br><br>_____ | **saber**<br><br>_____ |

Nombre _____ Hora _____

Fecha _____ **Vocabulary Check, Sheet 1**

Tear out this page. Write the English words on the lines. Fold the paper along the dotted line to see the correct answers so you can check your work.

cara a cara _____

la carta _____

comunicarse _____

_____

enviar _____

la tarjeta _____

bajar _____

buscar _____

la cámara
digital _____

la canción _____

la composición _____

la computadora
portátil _____

crear _____

el curso _____

la diapositiva _____

la dirección
electrónica _____

el documento _____

Fold In

**Realidades B**

**Capítulo 9B**

Nombre _____

Hora _____

Fecha _____

**Vocabulary Check, Sheet 2**

Tear out this page. Write the Spanish words on the lines. Fold the paper along the dotted line to see the correct answers so you can check your work.

face-to-face _____

letter _____

to communicate (with) _____

to send _____

card _____

to download _____

to search (for) _____

digital camera _____

_____

song _____

composition _____

laptop computer _____

_____

to create _____

course _____

slide _____

e-mail address _____

_____

document _____

Fold In →

**Realidades** **B**

**Capítulo 9B**

Nombre _____

Hora _____

Fecha _____

**Vocabulary Check, Sheet 3**

Tear out this page. Write the English words on the lines. Fold the paper along the dotted line to see the correct answers so you can check your work.

escribir por
correo electrónico _____
_____

estar en línea _____

grabar un disco
compacto _____

los gráficos _____

la información _____

el informe _____

el laboratorio _____

navegar en la Red _____

la presentación _____

el sitio Web _____

visitar salones
de chat _____

Fold In

Nombre _____

Hora _____

Fecha _____

Tear out this page. Write the Spanish words on the lines. Fold the paper along the dotted line to see the correct answers so you can check your work.

to send an
e-mail message _____
_____

to be online _____

to burn a CD _____
_____

graphics _____

information _____

report _____

laboratory _____

to surf the Web _____

presentation _____

Web site _____

to visit
chat rooms _____

To hear a complete list of the vocabulary for this chapter, go to Disc 2, Track 10 on the Guided Practice Audio CD, or go to www.phschool.com and type in the Web Code jcd-0999. Then click on **Repaso del capítulo**.

Fold In

# The present tense of *pedir* and *servir* (p. 320)

- You have learned other verbs with stem changes in the present tense (**pensar**, **querer**, **preferir**), where the stem changes from **e** to **ie**.
- **Pedir** (to *ask for*) and **servir** (to *serve, or to be useful for*) are also stem-changing verbs in the present tense, but their stem changes from **e** to **i**.
- Here are the present tense forms of **pedir** and **servir**. Notice that the **nosotros/nosotras** and **vosotros/vosotras** forms do not change their stem.

| yo | **pido** | nosotros/nosotras | **pedimos** |
|---|---|---|---|
| tú | **pides** | vosotros/vosotras | **pedís** |
| usted/él/ella | **pide** | ustedes/ellos/ellas | **piden** |

| yo | **sirvo** | nosotros/nosotras | **servimos** |
|---|---|---|---|
| tú | **sirves** | vosotros/vosotras | **servís** |
| usted/él/ella | **sirve** | ustedes/ellos/ellas | **sirven** |

**A.** Complete the chart with the correct forms of **pedir** and **servir**.

| | pedir | servir |
|---|---|---|
| **yo** | pido | |
| **tú** | | sirves |
| **Ud./él/ella** | | |
| **nosotros/nosotras** | | |
| **Uds./ellos/ellas** | | |

**B.** Write **e** or **i** in the blank to complete each verb form.

1. yo p____do
2. tú s____rves
3. nosotros s____rvimos
4. ellos p____den
5. Ud. s____rve
6. ellos s____rven
7. nosotros p____dimos
8. ella s____rve
9. yo s____rvo
10. tú p____des

# The present tense of *pedir* and *servir (continued)*

**C.** Circle the correct form of **pedir** or **servir** to complete each sentence.

1. Tú ( **sirve** / **sirves** ) café con leche y unas galletas.

2. Yo ( **pido** / **pedimos** ) una hamburguesa con papas fritas para el almuerzo.

3. Nosotros ( **pido** / **pedimos** ) un jugo de naranja.

4. Este libro ( **sirves** / **sirve** ) para aprender química.

5. Ellos ( **pedimos** / **piden** ) un tenedor limpio.

6. Todos los domingos mi madre ( **sirve** / **sirven** ) pescado para la cena.

7. Tú y yo ( **pido** / **pedimos** ) ayuda con la computadora.

8. Las computadoras ( **sirven** / **servimos** ) para conectar los sitios Web.

**D.** Write the correct form of the verb in the blank. Follow the model.

**Modelo** Yo siempre (**pedir**)_____ *pido* _____ yogur para el desayuno.

1. Mis amigos (**servir**) _____ café con el postre.

2. Nosotros siempre (**pedir**) _____ café con leche.

3. Las computadoras (**servir**) _____ para navegar la Red.

4. Tú y yo (**servir**) _____ jugo de naranja con una ensalada de frutas.

5. Tú siempre (**pedir**) _____ pizza para la cena.

6. Mis hermanos siempre (**pedir**) _____ huevos para el desayuno.

**E.** Complete the following sentences in a logical manner. Follow the models for ideas.

**Modelos** Los bolígrafos (**servir**)_____ *sirven para escribir* _____.

En el restaurante mexicano, yo siempre (**pedir**)_____ *pido enchiladas* _____.

1. Mi computadora (**servir**) _____

_____.

2. Para el desayuno, yo siempre (**pedir**) _____

_____.

3. Para el almuerzo, la cafetería siempre (**servir**) _____

_____.

4. Cuando vamos a un restaurante, mis amigos y yo (**pedir**) _____

_____.

**Go Online** WEB CODE jcd-0913 PHSchool.com

## *Saber* and *conocer* (p. 324)

- Both these verbs are irregular in the **yo** form only. Here are their present-tense forms.

| yo | **sé** | nosotros/nosotras | **sabemos** |
|---|---|---|---|
| tú | **sabes** | vosotros/vosotras | **sabéis** |
| usted/él/ella | **sabe** | ustedes/ellos/ellas | **saben** |

| yo | **conozco** | nosotros/nosotras | **conocemos** |
|---|---|---|---|
| tú | **conoces** | vosotros/vosotras | **conocéis** |
| usted/él/ella | **conoce** | ustedes/ellos/ellas | **conocen** |

**A.** Write the missing forms of **saber** and **conocer** in the chart.

| | saber | conocer |
|---|---|---|
| **yo** | sé | |
| **tú** | | |
| **Ud./él/ella** | | |
| **nosotros/nosotras** | | conocemos |
| **Uds./ellos/ellas** | | |

- Both **saber** and **conocer** mean *to know*.
- **Saber** means *to know how to do something* or *to know a fact*:
    Ella **sabe patinar**.     *She knows how to skate.*
    Él **sabe la respuesta**.     *He knows the answer.*
- **Conocer** means *to know a person* or *to be familiar with a place or thing*. Remember to use the personal **a** with **conocer** when it is used with a person.
    Ella **conoce Madrid**.     *She knows (is familiar with) Madrid.*
    Él **conoce a Miguel**.     *He knows Miguel.*

**B.** Look at each person, place, or thing. Write **S** if you would use **saber** or **C** if you would use **conocer**. Follow the model.

| Modelo | _S_ las matemáticas |
|---|---|

1. _____ la profesora de español
2. _____ nadar
3. _____ tocar la guitarra

4. _____ Tokyo
5. _____ Britney Spears
6. _____ la respuesta correcta

WEB CODE jcd-0914
PHSchool.com

*Guided Practice Activities* — 9B-3 **301**

**Realidades B**

**Capítulo 9B**

Nombre _____

Fecha _____

Hora _____

**Guided Practice Activities 9B-4**

# *Saber* and *conocer (continued)*

**C.** Circle the correct verb form of **conocer** in each sentence.

1. Yo ( **conoce** / **conozco** ) una tienda muy buena para comprar ropa.

2. Ellos ( **conoces** / **conocen** ) muy bien la ciudad de Nueva York.

3. Ella ( **conoce** / **conozco** ) a todos los estudiantes de la clase.

4. Tú y yo ( **conocemos** / **conozco** ) la música de Carlos Santana.

**D.** Circle the correct form of **saber** in each sentence.

1. Nosotros ( **saben** / **sabemos** ) hablar español.

2. Yo ( **sabe** / **sé** ) la respuesta correcta.

3. Tú ( **sabes** / **sabe** ) dónde está la clase de matemáticas.

4. Ud. ( **sabes** / **sabe** ) esquiar y nadar.

**E.** Complete each sentence with a form of **saber** or **conocer**. Circle the correct verb form according to the context.

1. Tú y yo ( **sabemos** / **conocemos** ) tocar el piano.

2. Ellas ( **saben** / **conocen** ) dónde están las llaves.

3. Yo ( **sé** / **conozco** ) al presidente de los Estados Unidos.

4. Tú ( **sabes** / **conoces** ) bien la ciudad de Chicago.

5. Ud. ( **sabe** / **conoce** ) usar la computadora nueva.

6. Nosotros ( **sabemos** / **conocemos** ) el nombre de una canción en español.

7. Tú ( **sabes** / **conoces** ) a todos los estudiantes de la clase.

8. Uds. ( **saben** / **conocen** ) a la estudiante nueva.

**F.** Complete the following sentences. Use ideas from the activities above or other words you know. Follow the model.

Modelo   Yo (saber) _____ *sé montar en bicicleta* _____ .

1. Yo (saber) _____ .

2. Yo no (saber) _____ .

3. Yo (conocer) _____ .

4. Yo no (conocer) _____ .

Go Online WEB CODE jcd-0914
PHSchool.com

**Realidades** **B**

**Capítulo 9B**

Nombre _____

Fecha _____

Hora _____

**Guided Practice Activities 9B-5**

## Lectura: La invasión del ciberspanglish (pp. 328–329)

**A.** The article in your textbook talks about the influence of computers on language. What computer terms can you think of in English? Write ten words or phrases that are commonly used when talking about the computer or the Internet. The first two have been done for you.

1.  _surf the Web_
2.  _to download_
3.  _____
4.  _____
5.  _____

6.  _____
7.  _____
8.  _____
9.  _____
10. _____

**B.** Did you find words in the reading similar to those on your list? You may have found the *ciberspanglish* words as well as the more correct Spanish terms for each word. Look on the chart in your reading and find the *ciberspanglish* and Spanish words for each.

|  | **Ciberspanglish** | **Español** |
|---|---|---|
| 1. to chat | _____ | _____ |
| 2. to reboot | _____ | _____ |
| 3. to program | _____ | _____ |
| 4. clip art | _____ | _____ |
| 5. to print | _____ | _____ |

**C.** Which list has the longer words in **part B**? Read the excerpts from the reading in your textbook. Then, write in English why some people want to use *ciberspanglish* terms and why some people prefer to use Spanish terms for computer-related words.

> *A algunas personas no les gusta nada este nuevo "idioma". Piensan que el español es suficientemente rico para poder traducir los términos del inglés.*
>
> *Hay otros que dicen que no hay problemas con mezclar los idiomas para comunicarse mejor. Piensan que el "ciberspanglish" es más fácil y lógico porque los términos técnicos vienen del inglés y expresarlos en español es bastante complicado.*

1.  It is better to use Spanish because _____
    _____.

2.  It is better to use *ciberspanglish* because _____
    _____.

Realidades **B**

**Capítulo 9B**

Nombre _____

Hora _____

Fecha _____

**Guided Practice Activities 9B-6**

# Presentación escrita (p. 331)

**Task:** Pretend that your parents think you spend too much time at the computer. Write an e-mail to a friend in Mexico defending your computer use.

**❶ Prewrite.** Fill in the chart below. In the first column, write in Spanish three ways you use the computer. In the second column, write the benefit (**ventaja**) to you. Use the first example as a guide.

| Cómo uso la computadora | La ventaja |
|---|---|
| Busco información para mis clases, en Internet. | Aprendo mucho y es muy interesante. |
| | |
| | |
| | |

**❷ Draft.** Use the information from the chart to write your e-mail.

**❸ Revise.** Before you have a partner review your work, check for spelling, accent marks, correct vocabulary use, and verb forms. Your partner will review the following:

_____ Is the paragraph easy to read and understand?

_____ Does the paragraph provide good reasons and support your position?

_____ Is there anything that you could add to give more information?

_____ Is there anything that you could change to make it clearer?

_____ Are there any errors that you missed?

**❹ Publish.** Rewrite the e-mail making any change suggested by your partner or by changing anything you didn't like.

**❺ Evaluation.** Your teacher will grade you on the following:

• the amount of information provided
• how well you presented each reason and its benefit
• your use of vocabulary and accuracy of spelling and grammar

# Notes

# Notes

# Notes

# Notes

# Notes

# Notes

# Notes

# Notes

Notes